A NEW OWNER'S
GUIDE TO
GOLDEN RETRIEVERS

JG-108

Overleaf: Adult and puppy Golden Retrievers owned by Paula Ashby and Lisa Smith.

Opposite page: This adorable Golden puppy is owned by Debbie and David Latino of Onital Goldens in Massachusetts.

The Publisher wishes to acknowledge the following owners of the dogs in this book: Paula M. Ashby, Nona Kilgore Bauer, Calypso Goldens, Ruth Coleman, Sharon Helstein Korncavage, Debbie and David Latino, Judy Laureano, James and Cindy Lichtenberger, Carol Lovejoy, Bruce R. MacCulloch, Julie A. MacKinnon, Kathy Martin, Kathy and Ted McCue, Barbara C. McKee, John Moore, the Morales family, Sue Mottley, Dorman and Alice Pantfoeder, Lisa Smith, Jim and Karen Taylor, Mary Vogler.

Photographers: Alverson Photographers, Inc., Mary Bloom, Isabelle Francais, Bruce K. Harkins, Dr. Kerry L. Ketring, Alice Pantfoeder, Robert Pearcy, Robert Smith, Judith E. Strom, Karen Taylor. Original art by John Quinn.

The author acknowledges the contribution of Judy Iby of the following chapters: Sport of Purebred Dogs, Identification and Finding the Lost Dog, Traveling with Your Dog, Health Care, Behavior and Canine Communication.

Distributed in the UNITED STATES to the Pet Trade by T.F.H. Publications, Inc., One T.F.H. Plaza, Neptune City, NJ 07753; distributed in the UNITED STATES to the Bookstore and Library Trade by National Book Network, Inc. 4720 Boston Way, Lanham MD 20706; in CANADA to the Pet Trade by H & L Pet Supplies Inc., 27 Kingston Crescent, Kitchener, Ontario N2B 2T6; Rolf C. Hagen Inc., 3225 Sartelon St. Laurent-Montreal Quebec H4R 1E8; in CANADA to the Book Trade by Vanwell Publishing Ltd., 1 Northrup Crescent, St. Catharines, Ontario L2M 6P5 ; in ENGLAND by T.F.H. Publications, PO Box 15, Waterlooville PO7 6BQ; in AUSTRALIA AND THE SOUTH PACIFIC by T.F.H. (Australia), Pty. Ltd., Box 149, Brookvale 2100 N.S.W., Australia; in NEW ZEALAND by Brooklands Aquarium Ltd. 5 McGiven Drive, New Plymouth, RD1 New Zealand; in Japan by T.F.H. Publications, Japan—Jiro Tsuda, 10-12-3 Ohjidai, Sakura, Chiba 285, Japan; in SOUTH AFRICA by Lopis (Pty) Ltd., P.O. Box 39127, Booysens, 2016, Johannesburg, South Africa. Published by T.F.H. Publications, Inc.
MANUFACTURED IN THE
UNITED STATES OF AMERICA
BY T.F.H. PUBLICATIONS, INC.

A New Owner's
Guide to
Golden Retrievers

Judy Laureano

Contents

Affectionate Goldens love attention from their owners.

Athletic Goldens often fare well in obedience trials.

Goldens are born with retrieving ability.

Active Golden puppies need to rest, too!

Versatile Goldens retrieve in water as well as on land.

PREFACE

Although I never had a pet until I was 23 years old, my life is now devoted to raising and caring for animals. I have been involved with the dog sport for 20 years, having started out in obedience with a white Miniature Poodle named Tasha. I then acquired a Golden Retriever instead of the German Shepherd I had promised my husband. Dolly, my first Golden, had a CDX and was trained through utility. Through her, we obtained our first dog who was to become a champion. Alphie led us to the breed ring and it is there that I have focused most of my attention for more than a decade. I owned the top winning Golden Retriever for 1986 and 1987: Ch. Laurell's Jiminy Crickett was one of the top winning Goldens in the history of the breed with 9 B.I.S., 5 B.I.S.S. and a foreign

The Golden Retriever is a breed which exemplifies beauty at any age. These Golden Retrievers are owned by the author.

Author Judy Laureano and her husband Ray with Ch. Laurell's Jiminy Crickett.

B.I.S to his credit. I have bred B.I.S. dogs and numerous champions. I enjoy judging match shows and hope one day to be a licensed judge. Currently I am owned by 14 Goldens, a Doberman, a P.B.G.V. and four cats. I also own and operate a commercial boarding kennel in Newfoundland, NJ. From having no pets, my life has certainly gone to the dogs.

INTRODUCTION to the Golden Retriever

Congratulations!! Why are you being congratulated? Well, you can only be reading this book for one of two reasons: either you have just decided on a Golden Retriever as a pet, in which case I congratulate you because you just made the best decision you have ever made in your entire life, or it might be that you are still undecided as to what type of pet would most suit you and your family, in which case I congratulate you because you have enough sense to make a Golden Retriever one of your final choices. There is no other breed of dog that is more loving, loyal or capable of bringing happiness into a family than a Golden. If you're not reading for one of the two reasons above, you can still keep on reading because this book will answer any questions you might have about Golden Retrievers.

The Golden Retriever emerged from a crossing of breeds meant to produce a strong, obedient dog that could be used by hunters to retrieve game.

ORIGIN OF THE GOLDEN RETRIEVER

To fully appreciate the Golden Retriever of today we have to look at how the breed has evolved over the years. Believe it or not, dogs were not always pets in the sense that we know them today. Early in his existence man learned that

This Golden puppy will never outgrow being playful and affectionate!

he could domesticate dogs and train them to help in hunting. By the 1300s, some of the dogs were refined enough to be separated into special breeds. Each breed exhibited specific hunting characteristics exclusive to that type of dog. For example, a spaniel was bred to flush, drive and chase game from the brush. Pointers and setters evolved to be used as pursuers of game that was flushed out and killed by hunters.

In the early 19th century, advances in weaponry helped hunters to bag more game, and therefore brought about the need for a durable retrieving dog.

By the 1830s, technological advances in weaponry made the sportsman capable of shooting more game in a day that he was previously able to. This led to a need for a dog that would retrieve all the game that was shot down during the day. This dog would have to be strong, energetic and durable because it was not uncommon for hunting parties to bag 1500 birds in one day. What the sportsmen were looking for was a dog that would retrieve, had a good nose and a soft mouth, was obedient and would not "range out" (run away and never come back).

To accomplish this goal, St. John's Newfoundlands, a variety of Newfoundland that was slimmer in build than what we know today and resembled a setter with the body of a Beagle, were crossed with retrieving setters. This crossing of breeds produced three new types of retrievers. The first kind was the Curly-Coated Retriever, the second was the Labrador Retriever and the third type was the Flat- or Wavy-Coated Retriever. This is the setting out of which the Golden Retriever emerged.

The Curly-Coated Retriever was one of the first breeds to result from the cross-breeding which would eventually produce the Golden Retriever.

For many years, it was believed that Goldens were descended from a troupe of Russian circus dogs. These dogs were believed to have been purchased by the first Lord Tweedmouth from which point they were taken to Guisachan, Scotland. The two greatest proponents of this theory were Colonel Hon le Poer Trench of St. Hubert's Kennel and Mrs. Charlsworth of Normandy Kennel. They did not have any proof, but as both were strong-minded and dictatorial, the theory took hold. The story that is told is that shortly after the Crimean War, Sir Dudley Majoriebanks, also known as the first Lord Tweedmouth, attended a circus in Brighton, Scotland. While there, he became very impressed with six Russian tracking dogs. He was especially drawn to their intelligence, cunning and golden color. He was in fact, so attracted that he supposedly bought the six dogs and returned them to his estate in Guisachan, Scotland where the dogs were used for hunting and tracking deer.

In 1883, Colonel le Poer Trench had obtained one of the descendants of the original Russian dogs from the Earl of Illchester, Lord Tweedmouth's nephew. He decided to keep his line pure from the Bloodhound strain, conveniently forgetting these dogs never had Bloodhound in them! The Colonel went to Russia to find some pure strain but failed. He then registered his dogs with the Kennel Club in England as the Majoriebanks and Illchester breed of "Yellow Russian Retrievers and Trackers," which was accepted by the Kennel Club as a separate breed.

When the Colonel died, his will instructed that all his dogs be put down. Mrs. Charlsworth carried on the story, saying that the gamekeeper at Guisachan remembered the Russian dogs arriving at the estate. The only slight evidence that this story may be true is that in Tweedmouth's stud book there is a dog noted in April of 1868 whose name was Sancho. That may be a circus name, but he was never used in the breeding program and he was never mentioned again in the book.

This was the story as people believed it until 1952 when the reputation of the breed was rescued by the dynamic duo of Elma Stonex and the Sixth Earl of

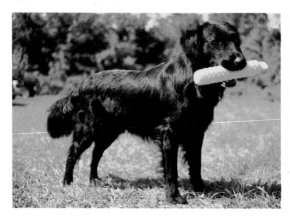

A yellow retriever from a litter of black Flat-Coated Retrievers produced four yellow puppies which became the foundation for the Golden Retriever.

Illchester. It seems that Lord Tweedmouth was not only a lord but also a careful geneticist who kept notes on his breeding practices. Tweedmouth was interested in animal husbandry and kept all sorts of cattle, horses and, of course, dogs. In 1865, Tweedmouth purchased his first yellow retriever from a litter of black, Wavy-Coated Retrievers. Understand that color was not fixed in the breed at that

These five-week-old Golden puppies are shining examples of the breed.

time, so it was not uncommon to see a yellow pup emerge from a breeding of two black dogs. The dog was named Nous and was bred to Belle, a Tweedwater Spaniel, in 1868. Now, in keeping with the age old adage—two great tastes that taste great together, Tweedwater saw characteristics in Nous and Belle that he wanted in one dog. Nous was an expert swimmer with a high level of endurance and Belle was a dog with a sweet and stable disposition. Tweedmouth left the two alone and let nature take its course. The resulting litter produced four yellow puppies: Crocus, Cowslip, Ada and Primrose. These four puppies were to become the foundation for the Golden Retriever.

Tweedmouth looked at his four pups and decided that he would keep Cowslip and Primrose. Crocus, the only dog of the litter, was given to Hon. Edward Majoriebanks, the second Lord Tweedmouth, and Ada was given to Lord Tweedmouth's nephew, the Earl of Illchester. Ada began the Illchester strain of Goldens, which was later called Melbury. Much loved by the Earl, Ada's gravestone can still be seen at the Illchester estate and is inscribed, "Ada with the Golden Hair."

Cowslip was the one puppy that was to enter the breeding program. She was paired up with a setter, which Tweedmouth believed would produce a dog with enhanced color and sharpened scenting abilities. Two puppies were kept from this mating, Jack and Gill. Cowslip, ever eager, was then bred again to a Tweedwater Spaniel. A puppy from this litter was bred to a black Flat- or Wavy-Coated Retriever named Sambo. (With me so far?) Now, a puppy from the resulting litter was kept in the breeding program, her name was Zoe. Zoe, in turn, was linebred back to Jack, Cowslip's son. (For those who have been following along, yes, Jack is Zoe's granduncle).

In looking for a breeding that would insure intense retrieving ability, Gill II was bred to Tracer, a black Flat-Coated Retriever. A litter of ten black puppies was produced. A female from that litter, Queenie, was bred back to Nous II. This litter produced two yellow puppies, Prim and Rose in 1889. What happened after that? Nobody knows exactly because Lord Tweedmouth died in 1894.

Early breeders of Golden Retrievers decided that they wanted to breed dogs with exceptional retrieving abilities— aptitude in and affinity for water was a must!

His recorded work was not carried on and Guisachan was sold in 1905. You might think that the story ends here, with the death of Tweedmouth and the termination of his recorded works, but it doesn't.

A man named Viscount Harcourt purchased two puppies from Guisachan. The dam was a bitch named Lady who was thought to be the daughter of Prim and Rose, the last recorded puppies from Tweedmouth's breeding program. How does this affect the breed today? Lady is listed as an ancestor to Calham Brass, and every Golden Retriever today can be traced back to Calham Brass. Because the first pedigrees of Tweedmouth's dogs were not registered until ten years after his death, it was very hard to connect Tweedmouth with today's Goldens. This last piece of information concerning Viscount Harcourt was the missing link. This link was found in the form of a letter mixed in with the possessions of Lady Pentland, the granddaughter of Lord Tweedmouth, who had been holding the kennel records. The letter was written by John MacLenna, a kennel keeper at Guisachan who stated that Viscount Harcourt bought his foundation stock from him.

The Golden Retriever, with his instinctive talent for retrieving, has come a long way from being thought of as the descendant of circus dogs in the 19th century.

As you can see, the Golden Retriever is a carefully planned canine, with certain attributes assured in the breed through years of conscious decision making on the part of owners. It would have been a shame if the breed continued to be thought of as a descendant of circus dogs. Thanks again to the work of Stonex and Illchester who uncovered the notes of Lord Tweedmouth, the English Kennel Club officially recognized the origin of the breed in 1960. The American Kennel Club and the Golden Retriever Club of America soon followed suit, thanks to the work of Rachael Page Elliot.

An interesting sidenote to the story of the breed's origin: the ruins of Guisachan and the original kennels of Lord Tweedmouth can be seen today. All Golden Retriever lovers who travel to Scotland should make it a "must see" part of their trip. It is in the vicinity of Loch Ness country and visitors can stay at Tomich House, a former hunting lodge.

GOLDEN RETRIEVERS IN NORTH AMERICA

Now you say, "Great, now I know how Golden Retrievers came into being" and you say, "Thank you, Lord Tweedmouth." But I bet you are wondering how Golden Retrievers came to America.

The earliest evidence there is of a Golden in North America is a picture taken in 1891 of Archie Majoriebanks, Tweedmouth's youngest son, at Rocking Chair Ranch in Texas. In the picture we see young Archie on a horse with a Golden Retriever at his feet. There are other pictures taken of Goldens in North America and all of them seem to be taken within the same time frame, between 1891 and 1900. However, the interest and breeding of Goldens did not begin in the United States until the 1930s.

The Golden craze in North America started in Canada. A man named Bart Armstrong established the first Golden Kennel in Winnipeg in 1918. He created the Gilnokie Kennel, which is responsible for many lines of today's Goldens. Later, Colonel S.S. Magoffin founded the Rockhaven Kennels in British Columbia and

Although a favorite breed in the United States today, the popularity of Golden Retrievers in North America started in Canada.

acquired Armstrong's Gilnokie Kennels, moving them to Inglewood, Colorado.

In Canada, the Golden Retriever was recognized as being a separate breed in 1927 and in turn was registered with the Canadian Kennel Club. The first Golden Retriever registered with the American Kennel Club was Lomberdale Blondin in 1925. It was not until 1930, when Colonel Magoffin imported the excellent dog Ch. Speedwell Pluto, that the public's interest in Goldens began to grow. Ch. Speedwell Pluto went onto become the first Golden Retriever to win Best in Show in Puget Sound, Washington in 1933. With the infusion of Speedwell Pluto and Rockhaven Kennels into North America, the interest in Golden Retrievers began in earnest.

The breed continued to grow mainly in the Midwest, where most of the kennels were located. The Minnesota area boasted the location where the majority of influential kennels opened their doors. Kennels like Silroven in Winnona, Minnesota; Pirates Den in Rochester, Minnesota; Goldwood Kennels in White Bear

Lake, Minnesota; and Tanahoff Kennel in Minneapolis, Minnesota were dual purpose kennels. These kennels would breed Goldens to perform in both field and conformation championships. Also worthy of mention are Taramar Kennels, Featherquest Kennels and Golden Knolls Kennels. Dogs from all these kennels can be found in any of today's pedigrees. These are the dogs and people who established, promoted and protected the Golden Retriever in its early development in the U.S. As the breed and its popularity increased, so have the people who devote their time to the breeding of this lovely animal. Today one can find Golden Retriever breeders in every area of the country. These breeders continue to improve and protect the Golden Retriever.

The Golden Retriever Club of America

As the Golden Retriever became more popular, it followed that people who were involved with the breed would come together for companionship and shared information. In 1930, the Golden Retriever Club of America was founded. This organization has continued to grow since its inception and nearly every state has a Golden Retriever club affiliated with the G.R.C.A. Each club holds its own breed shows, obedience trials and hunting events.

One of the events that Golden fanciers look forward to annually is the "National," which is held in different parts of the country each year. It is a showcase of the Golden Retriever's breed qualities along with obedience and hunting abilities. It is also a place where the owners of Golden Retrievers can talk about Goldens to their hearts' content. The National is a wonderful source of information about the breed for new Golden owners. When you register your dog, you will receive information on the G.R.C.A. Take the time to read it and, if it suits you, get involved in a local club. If you decided that you do not want to get involved in the shows, but you still want to contact other Golden owners for support and consultation, call the American Kennel Club. The club will send you information on your local Golden Retriever Club. The G.R.C.A. is also recognized as one of the most involved clubs in the U.S. in the area of public education, pioneering the P.A.L. letter that went out with all new Golden Retriever registrations from the A.K.C. and that the A.K.C. has adopted and is now using in its own literature. It also contributes monetarily to health research, supporting research on cancer in dogs, on subaortic stenosis (S.A.S.) and many other canine related health problems.

From a single registered Golden Retriever in 1925, this breed has grown to become one of the most popular dogs in the United States. Everywhere you look today you can see a Golden Retriever: they are on T.V., in the magazines, in shopping catalogues or out walking with their human companions. Golden Retrievers are noble, intelligent and wonderful dogs. Let us hope that today's breeders can continue to keep all the qualities that Lord Tweedmouth wanted in his "yellow retrievers."

The Golden Retriever possesses many characteristics which make him a wonderful all-around sporting dog and human companion.

CHARACTERISTICS of the Golden Retriever

Lord Tweedmouth's careful breeding and the generations of careful and conscientious breeders that followed Lord Tweedmouth have given us today's Golden Retrievers. They are some of the most gentle, noble, intelligent and beautiful dogs today. Once you have owned a Golden, no other breed will ever take its place in your heart. Still willing and able to do the job they were originally bred for, Golden Retrievers make quick and enthusiastic gun dogs. They have consistently taken top honors in obedience competitions. Because of their wonderful temperament, they are used as therapy dogs to visit the sick and elderly. Their success as guide dogs for the blind and companion dogs for the handicapped is renowned.

One of the most popular dogs in the United States today, one only has to come in contact with someone who owns a Golden Retriever to hear endless platitudes on the positive attributes that accompany the breed. They are smart; each of us has at least one "smart Golden" story to tell. Each of us has the most beautiful Golden, each of us has a clown who loves to make us laugh, each of us has a best friend, each of us has a loyal, loving, intelligent, unselfish, beautiful, funny, smart

Goldens consistently fare well in competition— Glorybee Darling Dundee, UD, competes in agility.

Golden. Once you bring a Golden Retriever into your family, you must remember that you do not own him; it is the Golden Retriever who owns you.

Energetic yet gentle, Golden Retrievers are ideal pets for families with children.

BREED OVERVIEW

Fairly easy to train and housebreak, Goldens are easy dogs to integrate into your home. Their love of people makes them easy to have in a house full of children. Their love of water and athletic ability make them wonderful companions for the owner who loves nature or again

The Golden Retriever's versatility and adaptability truly make him a "dog for all seasons."

for children who love to play ball and go swimming. They are also content to sleep at your feet on a cold winter night. I haven't met a Golden who dislikes a warm bed.

They are sporting dogs and do need a certain amount of exercise. This can be in the form of a walk in the park, a game of fetch, a swim in a pond or a session in dog playgroups, which are popular in the larger cities around the country. It should, however, consist of a steady walk and not a "window shopping" walk. If at all possible, you should find some enclosed area where your dog can be taken "off lead" or let loose to run and enjoy some freedom. Letting your dogs out in the backyard may not be sufficient exercise, as they seem to only sit at the door waiting to be let back into the house.

This quickly-growing Golden pup will soon be too big to sit comfortably in his owner's lap.

Because they are a double-coated breed, the undercoat keeping them warm and dry, Goldens have at least two very heavy sheds a year: one in the spring and one in the fall. Both of these sheds produce a tremendous amount of hair. While brushing during this time helps, it is almost impossible to keep your house hair-free. One thing to remember is that a double coat and heavy shedding does not make a Golden the perfect pet for someone with allergies.

The average Golden male is between 70 and 80 pounds thus making him a medium-sized dog. One must be aware that the cute ten-pound puppy that is brought into the home will grow very fast and in nearly six months he will be a gangly puppy of 40 to 50 pounds. While good around young children and babies, the dog must be taught how to respect and

Children should be taught to treat their family pets with care and respect. Here, Alexis and Roxie seem to be getting along well!

treat the children and vice-versa. Kids must learn how the dog is to be treated in order to prevent any unfortunate accidents.

HEALTH CONCERNS FOR THE BREED

As the popularity of the Golden Retriever increases, so do the health problems in the breed. The main health concerns in our breed are hip dysplasia, cataracts and subartoic stenosis (S.A.S.).

Hip Dysplasia

This is a genetic disease that is characterized by a malformation of the hip joint, which in its most severe form can be crippling and painful for the dog. In order to prevent the passage of this gene from generation to generation, Golden Retrievers that are used in breeding programs must have clearance on their hips either from Orthopedic Foundation for Animals or Penn-Hip. The more generations of "clear" dogs that a breeder can show you, the better your chances of buying a puppy that will not be affected by hip dysplasia. Remember though, as with any genetic disease, hip dysplasia can appear at any time.

Cataracts

A cataract is an opacity in the eye. The most common form in Goldens is a juvenile cataract. Again, breeding

X-rays are used to detect hip dysplasia, a genetic disease which is one of the main health concerns in Golden Retrievers.

stock is examined yearly by a board-certified group of ophthalmologists, and only dogs who clear this exam should be bred. Juvenile cataracts can continue to grow and eventually lead to blindness, although this is very rare.

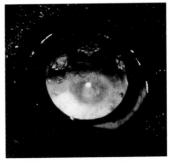

Immature cataract—the pupil in this two-year-old dog has been dilated for examination. The central white area and cloudy areas represent the cataract.

Subartoic Stenosis

This is a hereditary disease of the heart in which the muscle ring around the aorta continues to grow, narrowing the aorta. As the aorta narrows it builds tremendous pressure in the heart. In the most severe cases, the dog's heart gives out and he dies very suddenly and without warning. A disease that is relatively new in Golden Retrievers, it varies in severity. S.A.S. can cause sudden death at a young age or a dog with S.A.S. can lead a long, normal life. Breeding stock should be examined by a board-certified cardiologist before one year of age and again at two years of age. ONLY cleared stock should be used for breeding.

There are other health concerns in Goldens that, while not as serious, you should be aware of. We are seeing an increase in dogs with allergies, thyroid problems, bone problems and, as with every breed, a great increase in the incidence of cancer, not only in the older dog but in the younger dog as well. You should discuss these problems with the people you buy your puppy from and find out if these health problems are showing up in their breeding program.

When deciding on a Golden Retriever puppy, be aware of the health problems. Purchase your puppy from someone willing to show you all of the appropriate clearances on both the mother and father.

SPECIAL ROLES in Today's Society

Golden Retrievers can be seen in almost every walk of life; they seem to be trained for almost any task. They are used as guide dogs for the blind. In fact, some centers for the blind have their own Golden breeding programs. They also are being used extensively in the companion dog program. This is a program where dogs are trained to do whatever a handicapped person needs to have done. Dogs are taught to open cupboards, turn on lights, carry packages and do anything else the person needs help with in everyday life. They have also been used as hearing dogs, signaling to the owner when the doorbell or phone rings.

The Golden's friendly nature makes him a good therapy dog.

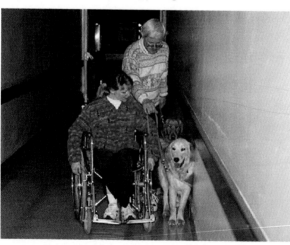

We see Goldens pictured in the newspapers doing search and rescue work. They are excellent at this task and it is something that, if you are interested in, you can train the dog to do yourself. Most search and rescue dogs are owned by individuals who form search and rescue groups. When authorities need the help of the search and rescue teams, they call in

Since Golden Retrievers are easy to train and take directions well, they often win obedience titles.

the dogs. Goldens are used in drug enforcement at the local and federal levels. The first drug dog used at the Statue of Liberty was a Golden Retriever. They are used in arson investigations and as bomb dogs. It seems as if there is no task that a Golden Retriever cannot perform.

I don't have to tell you the popularity of the breed in advertising. We only have to turn on the T.V. or pick up a magazine or catalog and there is that wonderful Golden face looking at us. They are friendly and easy to train, and very few people can be afraid of a face that looks so kind with large dark eyes that have nothing but trust in them. Walk down a street and you will find yourself drawn to these beautiful yellow dogs. They have invaded every aspect of our society and can be trained for anything. Famous obedience dogs have graced the breed with the first three dogs ever to win obedience titles being Golden Retrievers. There are famous hunting Goldens and plenty of stories of Golden Retrievers saving the life of hunters. Let us not forget Liberty, the Golden Retriever who lived in the White House with President Gerald Ford.

Golden Retrievers are often used as companion dogs for the handicapped. The dogs are trained to help their companions in all aspects of everyday life.

Another manifestation of Goldens' ability and temperament is the use of them in therapy programs. Therapy dogs are certified animals that are allowed to go into nursing homes and long-term care facilities. They do nothing more than visit the patients, give the patients the opportunity to pet them and generally keep the patients company. The beneficial effects of this program are well documented as the therapy dogs serve as surrogate pets to the people in hospitals. There are numerous accounts of patients talking only to these dogs or taking an interest in an otherwise hopeless life because of the companionship a pet will provide. The Golden Retriever, because of his temperament, is an excellent dog for this type of work. Therapy work is another thing that the average owner can get involved in. It is rewarding for you as well as your dog. To find out more about the program in your area, call a local nursing home and see if they offer a therapy dog program. They will be glad to give you the name and number of the contact person.

Because of their good looks, trainability, intelligence and temperament, Golden Retrievers are among the most beloved dogs in this country. It is up to each of us that owns or, as I like to say, is owned by a Golden Retriever to protect and promote all that is good in the breed.

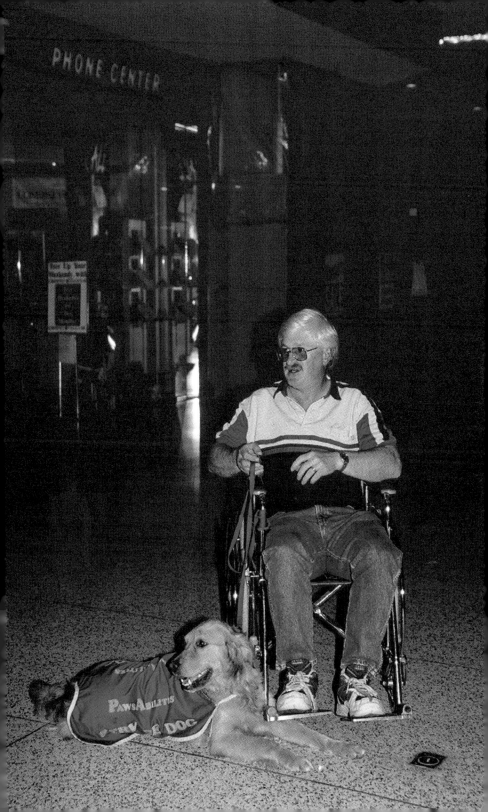

STANDARD for the Golden Retriever

As each breed is recognized by the American Kennel Club it is given a standard or a guideline that ensures that it will essentially remain the same from generation to generation. For the Golden Retriever, height and weight, color, shape of head and body, eyes, movement and temperament all are included in the breed standard as guidelines for the breeder so the basic dog remains the same. Within that standard there is free interpretation and it is this freedom to interpret that gives us the many different types of Golden Retrievers. This is why there are light Goldens and dark Goldens, big heads and small heads. However, all these different types fall within the standard and all the types are recognized as Golden Retrievers.

The Golden Retriever's alert, friendly disposition should be evident in his expression and in his eyes.

SKULL AND HEAD

The Golden Retriever is a powerful, active dog. He should be neither clumsy nor leggy and display a soft, loyal expression with a self confident, alert, eager personality. His head should be wide in back skull with a well-defined stop. The stop is the part of the skull between the

The wide-in-back skull, well-defined stop, slightly tapering muzzle, and firm jowls are defining points of the Golden Retriever's head.

eyes where the snout and muzzle begin. His muzzle (mouth and nose) should be between 6 and 8 inches and should be slightly narrower at the tip than at the stop. The jowls, or the skin that hangs over the mouth on both sides of the skull, should not be heavy or droopy. The correct bite for a Golden is a scissors-type bite. The lower teeth should be set slightly behind the upper teeth. The nose should be black or brownish black, although in the colder weather it sometimes fades to brownish pink. A pink nose is not acceptable. This does not mean that your Golden will not be able to register with the A.K.C., it just means he will not win many championships in the show ring. The ears should be rather short, attached just above and behind the eyes. When you pull the ear forward it should just cover the eye. His eyes give him

The Golden's body is powerful and athletic; his tail thick and muscular. This dog holds his tail curved slightly upward—it should never be held between the legs.

The Golden should have a dense, straight coat that may be wavy, though not curly. Shades of gold are acceptable provided that there are no white markings.

away as a friendly and intelligent dog. The rims of the eyes should be close fitting and the eyes themselves should be dark brown in color. They should be medium large and slightly almond shaped.

BODY

The Golden possesses a powerful body, well balanced and athletic. In the standard, each part of the body is discussed and the ideal formation is given. It discusses leg placement, shoulder formation and how things should be put together. One of the more common facets of the standard is size of the feet, which are medium sized, round and compact. Another part of the body that the standard addresses is the tail, which should be thick and muscular. It should be carried level to the back or curved slightly upward. The tail should never be curled over the back or held between the legs.

COAT

The coat should be dense with a good undercoat. It should not be coarse or silky. The coat should lie close to the body and may be straight and wavy, but not curly. Remember that these dogs were bred for retrieving in all types of environments—warm, cold, wet or dry—and for that reason their coats should not be excessively heavy. The color of the coat, as stated in the standard, is a "rich, lustrous gold of various shades. Feathering maybe lighter than the rest of the coat." There should be no white markings on a Golden Retriever.

MOVEMENT

Because the Golden Retriever is a hunting dog, his movement is important, an issue that is addressed in the standard. He should have an easy, free movement, with his front legs having good reach or extension at the same time his rear legs are driving him forward. The faster the dog moves the more tendency he should have to "converge to a center line of balance." He should be a powerful mover, able to cover ground seemingly without effort nor should he tire easily. He is a level mover, his legs moving in a straight line, turning neither in nor out. Some common faults are feet that turn in or out, or toeing in or out. Elbows that appear to "stick out" at the

In normal circumstances, a Golden Retriever should not show aggression or fear toward people or other dogs.

side or that seem to stick out when the dog moves is called winging. A dog can move "too close in the rear," meaning, from the hocks down, the legs are too close together or "sickle hocked." He can stand "cow-hocked," which means he looks bow-legged and this will interfere with his rear driving motion.

Movement is one of the characteristics judged in the show ring.

HEIGHT AND WEIGHT

The Golden standard also has height and weight qualifications. The males are 23-24" at the withers or shoulders and females are 21.5-22.5" at the withers with an inch above or below the standard being acceptable. Deviation of more than an inch in either direction is a disqualifying fault. Weight for dogs is 65-75 pounds, for bitches the weight standard is 55-65 pounds.

TEMPERAMENT

Temperament is also spelled out in the standard and is of the utmost importance today. The standard states, "Temperament-friendly, reliable and trustworthy. Quarrelsomeness or hostility toward other dogs or people in normal situations or unwarranted shows of timidity or nervousness is not in keeping with the Golden Retriever character." This issue is one of the biggest concerns. We must diligently keep in mind what Golden Retrievers are supposed to be and continue to breed "friendly, reliable and trustworthy" dogs.

OVERALL VIEW

We should keep in mind when we are judging a Golden Retriever that no perfect dog has ever been born. We should not "fault judge," but rather look at the overall dog. His proportions, balance and overall soundness are more important than his individual faults.

CHOOSING a Golden Retriever

Now let's say you've made your choice and concluded that the only way to make your life complete is to invite a Golden Retriever into your house. What is the next step? Well, let's ask some difficult questions:

Where do you want to purchase your puppy?

What are you looking for in a puppy?

What is your budget?

Do you want a male or a female?

Do you want a show dog, a dog for obedience, a dog for hunting or just a family dog?

Perhaps the best way to get help on answering these questions is to first read all the available books on the Golden Retriever.

People who own Golden Retrievers can be great sources of information for the prospective Golden owner.

Each has its own view and information on the breed. When you feel like you have a grasp on the breed, its good and bad points and its health problems, call the A.K.C. From the A.K.C. you can get the name of the nearest "puppy referral" person in your area. A "puppy referral" person will give you a list of breeders who will be willing to answer all of your questions. You might even get an invitation to come and visit the kennel

Once you've decided that the Golden Retriever is the breed for you, the search for the perfect puppy (or adult dog) can begin!

where you will be able to see adults and puppies. This experience would be good for anyone who has never owned a Golden. You would be able to see all the stages that a Golden goes through on his way to adulthood.

Another recommendation I have to help you decide if the Golden is the right dog for you is to find out about local dog shows and obedience trials. The shows are an excellent place to see the breed in action. Many Golden owners bring their puppies and adult dogs to these shows so it is a great place to view the breed at its best. The shows are also a great place to meet many of the people behind the breed. Breeders and owners are the best people to ask any questions you might have since most owners have been around Goldens for a long time. Go, watch and ask questions. Decide on a type, decide on what you really want—male, female, show, pet, working. Get some opinions from different breeders. Afterwards, start your search for the right dog for you.

SELECTING A BREEDER

The next step for potential owners would be to go to a breeder who has a litter of puppies on the grounds. From this visit you should use your common sense to see if this is a breeder that you want to buy your puppy from. There are a few guidelines that should be followed. Minimally, all Goldens that are used in a breeding program should have hip clearances from OFA or Penn-Hip, an eye clearance from a board-

A potential Golden owner should visit a breeder who has a litter of puppies. The young Golden should look healthy and active like these playful pups!

certified ophthalmologist and a heart clearance from a board-certified cardiologist.

As for the intangibles for which common sense judgments should be used, you should be able to see the mother and judge her reaction to you, judge her interaction with the puppies and check her condition to see if she looks healthy. Keep in mind that the stress of whelping and nursing a litter of puppies can take its toll on the mother. She may look thin and will definitely be shedding her coat. She may not look like the beautiful girl you saw in the show ring.

Puppies should be kept in a warm, clean area where they are exposed to people and to the noises and activity of daily life.

You should also concern yourself with the condition of the puppies themselves. They should have room to move around. The area they are kept in should be clean and warm. The puppies should be in a location where they are able to see and hear the day to day action in the household. Puppies that are more exposed to people, noises and voices will be better socialized and better able to handle the transition from the breeder's to your home.

Also, you should judge the puppies' physical appearance. They should seem plump, and their coats should be fluffy and thick. Their eyes should be clear and bright. There should be no sign of parasites, fleas or worms. The first set of shots should have been administered and a clean bill of health from a vet should be available to you.

There is also the question of personality in your potential puppy. Puppies should be curious about their surroundings, not shy and withdrawn. Puppies are naturally curious and should explore the area around them. Inquisitiveness about noises, people and other puppies is also a sign of a mentally healthy puppy. Good breeders will have observed the puppies and their personality. This observation should enable them to help you pick a puppy that best suits your lifestyle. They should also be very willing to continue to guide you and answer any questions you have after you leave with your puppy.

MALE OR FEMALE?

When looking for puppies, another question frequently asked is "What is better, male or female?" In Golden Retrievers the difference is only in the size of the dogs, with females being a little smaller. The temperament in both dogs is very similar. My vote, though, goes to males who seem to me to have a sweeter, more steady temperament. I do not find that the males wander or "mark" everything, nor do they try to escape.

Females, unless they are spayed, will go into season two times a year. A bitch's full season lasts 21 days and is divided into three stages. During the first stage she will have a light flow of blood with the color going from bright red to a straw color. In the beginning the male will be only mildly interested in her. She will have no interest in him. As the blood becomes straw colored, the flow will slow down and the male will be very interested in her and she in him.

It is now that breeding and conception will take place. This should also be the time of extreme caution for breeders and owners. Don't let dogs and "in season" bitches mingle unless you want a litter of puppies. This stage occurs nine to 15 days after the first sign of blood. In the last stage the blood will turn red again and there will be little interest between the two dogs. Either just before or just after her season, the female will "blow" or shed out her coat, thus adding two more heavy sheds a year.

For the average pet owner, I feel that temperament, type and color are more important than the sex of the dog. The Golden Retriever is one breed where sex truly doesn't make a difference.

While we are discussing male vs. female, this is a good time to talk a little bit about spaying and neutering. If you have decided to purchase a show dog, then spaying or neutering cannot be considered. However, if you have decided that your puppy will be a pet, then you should definitely spay or neuter your dog. Health-wise, it is the best thing to do for your dog as the incidence of mammary cancer and prostate cancer drop to almost zero, especially if it is done before your puppy reaches six months of age. Conveniently, when a female is spayed, you won't have to deal with her "seasons."

Sex and temperament are things to consider as you set out to find the right Golden Retriever for you.

In males, neutering insures that they stay away from unwanted behaviors, such as territorial tendencies. It does not affect them in any adverse way. Males do not become "fat and lazy" after being neutered; if anything, it improves their ability to be good pets since they do not have to cope with hormonal changes.

ADOPTING AN ADULT GOLDEN RETRIEVER

What do you do if you have decided on a Golden Retriever as a pet but you realize that your lifestyle is not one where you have the time to train a new puppy. You are not home during the day, your schedule hinders your ability to correctly housetrain a puppy, you don't want to spend an exorbitant amount of money on a new puppy, or you want to travel and you can't do that with a puppy in your life; whatever the reason, do not be discouraged from getting a Golden Retriever. For the person that can't fit a puppy into their lifestyle, there is always the option of adopting an adult Golden Retriever. Almost every state has some sort of Golden Retriever rescue that takes adult dogs out of shelters or from people who can no longer care for their pets and places them in homes where puppies are not always the best choice. These rescue dogs are usually spayed or neutered, have all their shots and have been evaluated in terms of personality and appropriateness of placement. A rescue dog will be evaluated so that the right dog ends up with the right people. The adoption process for a rescue is similar to the adoption process for children. At the very least, there will be an adoption form to fill out and some type of home visit to potential adopters. There are also adoption fees. This is a wonderful way for you to get a Golden and it is also a great way to give a dog a second chance. These dogs desperately need homes; if a puppy doesn't suit your lifestyle, please consider the rescue program as an option. The Golden Retriever Club

of America maintains a list of people and phone numbers of adoption services across the country.

Another excellent way to obtain an older

If raising a puppy doesn't quite fit your lifestyle, consider adopting an adult Golden Retriever.

Adult Goldens can be adopted through shelters and rescue missions, or from breeders who place their older dogs with loving families.

dog is through breeders. Often times, a dog that does not obtain his clearances (eyes, hips, heart) will be placed. They can not be used in a breeding program but will make wonderful pets. Also, many breeders will place dogs that are in the four- to eight-year-old range for various reasons, the main one being that the breeder may just have too many dogs. It could also be possible that the dog has grown tired of the show ring and the owner just wants to provide the dog with a good home with its own special family. Again, they will be neutered or spayed and have all of their shots. This method may take longer but often times is worth the wait. Both of these methods of obtaining an older dog are well worth looking into. It is a wonderful way to give your heart to a Golden Retriever.

PREPARING for Your New Puppy

You have found the right breeder, you have found the right litter, you are comfortable with the choice you have made regarding sex. You have seen the litter at least twice and you have picked out your puppy.

The day has come for you to bring the puppy home. You have done your homework, chosen the housebreaking method you feel you will have the most success with and you have found a veterinarian whom you trust. You have found and purchased the same kind of food the puppy is currently being fed. You

Your new puppy will be apprehensive at first—it is your job to welcome him to his new home.

have toys—lots of toys, you have a leash and collar, you have eating and drinking bowls and you have rehearsed the kids. When the puppy comes home, you must remember that this will be the first time he is away from his littermates. He may be apprehensive about his new surroundings. In order to try and ease the transition for the pup, keep things calm around him. This is not the time to have a welcome home puppy party. Take him outside and let him get used to you and his new surroundings. Remember to keep it low-key. It may take a couple of days for the puppy to adjust so be patient and calm with him.

Perhaps the first night you should have him sleep with you so he can be reassured if he starts to cry. A stuffed toy to cuddle with will help suppress his feelings of loneliness. As he grows accustomed to you, introduce him to new things and new settings. A walk to the school bus and a trip to the kids' football game are great ways to socialize the puppy. What you want to do most of all is take the puppy out so he can see different things, meet different people and get involved

Training and socializing your puppy at a young age will help him grow into a well-behaved, well-adapted adult dog.

in different situations. Your goal should be to have a well adjusted, social dog that takes all experiences in stride.

One of the things that most owners find surprising with Golden Retriever puppies is their rapid rate of growth. Get ready for this sudden growth spurt. Most Goldens start out life at about 1 pound and by the time they are 1 year old weigh between 60-70 pounds. This one year life span takes the dog through the infant stage, toddler years, teenage years and young adulthood with rapid increases in size accompanying all stages.

Understanding this physical and mental growth can help you face the challenges of raising a puppy. Once again, I suggest that you read, read, read. There are many methods of training. It is up to you to decide which would be best for you and your puppy.

TAKE ME TO YOUR ALPHA

The main thing to remember when raising a puppy is that you must become the Alpha, or dominant person, in that dog's life. Dogs have been domesticated for thousands of years, but they are still descended from wolves. Wolves are pack animals and, as with every pack, there must be a leader. Dogs will look for the leader and if none is present, will gladly step into the role. Your job is to become the Alpha. You must establish a chain of dominance and demonstrate it to the puppy. Now, a dominant person does not mean that you beat, bully

Integrating a new puppy into your family often means teaching him to get along with the other family pets.

or yell at the dog; however, it does mean that you are firm and consistent in dealing with the puppy. Most puppies will respond to a firm "no." They will easily recognize that a person who says "no" 20 times but does nothing to enforce the reprimand is not the alpha and he will gladly step in to take over that role.

LIKE A WORK OF ART

Have a picture of how you would like your adult dog to behave and then create the image by training the dog at a young age. If you don't want a 70-pound dog on your furniture, don't let the puppy on the furniture; if you don't want an adult dog jumping on guests, don't let a puppy jump on guests. Start out right by being firm and consistent with your young dog. Take time out to train the puppy and you will have a well-behaved adult Golden Retriever that has learned manners, is willing to accept new situations and has learned his position in the family.

If you find there is a habit the puppy has that you can't break or he is starting to exhibit unwanted behavior, call the breeder. It is important that you call the breeder and get some advice before the problem goes beyond something that you alone can handle. Don't wait for the behavior to become a major problem that threatens your happiness and the happiness of the dog.

Sometimes a training method that you have chosen does not work with the puppy you have. If that situation occurs, be willing to switch methods to something that might make the dog more responsive to your wishes. There will come a time in the first year when the puppy will decide to challenge your authority, much as a teenager does. Remember that you have laid the groundwork as to what type of pet you will have. Your dog knows what to expect from you and he knows what is expected of him. This is where your firmness and

Which one is the real *puppy? Fluffy, cute Golden puppies often resemble cuddly teddy bears.*

consistency will pay off; the firm "no" will make the puppy remember that you are in charge, you are the Alpha and he must obey you. This will make the beginning stages of training relatively easy to get through.

PHYSICAL GROWTH

The Golden Retriever reaches physical maturity anywhere from one year old to three years old.

You lay the foundation for your dog's behavior—firm and consistent training will result in an obedient dog.

Your Golden Retriever will go through many physical changes as he makes the transition from cute puppy to regal adult.

Maximum height is reached at around one year but muscle and physique continue to develop for at least another year. Their bodies are constantly changing in that first year; that cute "teddy bear" puppy you brought home is

suddenly a gangly four-month-old. He is all legs and feet with teeth falling out and he no longer has that fluffy baby coat but is beginning to show signs of a "real" Golden coat. Keep the coat brushed and you will have less of it flying around your house. Check his mouth and make sure the baby teeth are coming out. Sometimes what will happen is that the permanent teeth will start to come in but the baby teeth will not be pushed out. If you check your puppy's mouth and it looks as if this is happening, call your vet, explain the problem and take his advice as to what your next course of action should be.

Something that might seem silly at first but will help your dog in the long run is brushing his teeth. Dogs can contract gum disease as easily as people can; brushing of the dog's teeth will lessen the chances that your puppy will have problems later on in his adult life. Start when the dog is young so that he gets used to the procedure. You might ask, "What type of toothpaste do I use?" You should use some sort of special dog toothpaste that is available in most pet stores.

At some point in the first year the puppy will "blow" or shed out his puppy coat. You'll probably think that he is going bald and wonder why it looks like dog hair is falling from your ceiling. If you're the type of person who doesn't like dog hair all over your house, maybe you

Gumabone® products, like the Gumabone® Frisbee®*, are great chew toys for teething puppies. The trademark Frisbee is used under license from Mattel, Inc., CA, USA.

shouldn't have a Golden Retriever, but, if you do, the best way to prevent such inconveniences is to have a brush handy at all times. When you brush your puppy, use long strokes and brush through to the skin. This will also be a trying time; remember to brush your puppy often and you will eventually get through it. After the baby coat goes, the adult Golden coat should start to come in. Within two to four months your puppy will look like an adult.

It is natural for a young Golden Retriever to be curious and inquisitive. This puppy investigates the contents of his water bowl.

EMOTIONAL GROWTH

While your Golden physically does most of his growing in the first year, his emotional maturity will take another year. You will find at two years old it seems to "all come together." He will calm down and be ready to listen all the time. He will understand his position in the family and what is expected of him. In short, he will be the perfect Golden Retriever. Each stage your puppy goes through will bring joy and frustration. Enjoy the good parts, enjoy his cuteness, his inquisitiveness, his adventures, his misadventures, his comic antics, his awakenings and his lack of social skills. When the going gets tough and he seems to have unlearned everything you have taught him, stick to the firmness and consistency with which you have trained him. He will eventually fit into the mold you have created for him and he will be the perfect Golden Retriever. Do not, however, get so caught up in the discipline that you lose sight of the special times that can be had between you and your pet.

HOUSEBREAKING Your Golden Retriever

Golden Retrievers have become known as one of the easiest and most adaptive of all breeds. They like to please, they like to be in your good graces, and if you show them what you want and are firm with them, their responses are quick.

The most accepted means of housebreaking is crate training. Many people's reaction is, "I don't want to put my dog in a cage." These worries are based more on what human beings find comfortable than what is instinctive for the dog. If we remember the wolf, from which all dogs are descended, we find that it is a den animal. It is instinctive for dogs to find enclosed spaces to rest, sleep and relax. If you watch most dogs, you will not find them laying in open spaces but rather you will find them sleeping under desks or tables or curled up on the floor next to the sofa. They are most comfortable in an enclosed area.

If you keep your dog in a crate and housebreak him in a crate, you will find that your job will be much easier. Dogs are also very clean animals and will not soil their sleeping and eating areas. Keeping your puppy in a crate will just compliment his natural tendency to keep his "home" clean.

The basic rule of crate training is to make the puppy think the crate is his home. The puppy should remain in the crate unless somebody is with him. The puppy should be fed in the crate. Everything the puppy does, aside from playing, exercising and being with the family should take place in the crate. If this procedure is followed, the puppy will realize that the crate is a safe haven, a comfortable place for him to relax. It becomes his house. Of course, the puppy must be taken out every few hours but he soon learns his schedule. Within three weeks you should have a puppy that is on a schedule, that knows when it is time to go outside and knows not to use the house as his bathroom.

A puppy must be taken out after every meal. How long after the puppy finishes eating? Usually about 15 minutes is a good amount of time to wait before you take the puppy for a walk. When the puppy does "go," remember to praise him and tell him how wonderful he is. If he then comes in from his walk and plays for another 15 minutes, it is usually a good idea to take him out again. The activity can get his system going and he will be ready to eliminate again.

The puppy must be taken out as soon as someone wakes up in the morning. This means as soon as someone wakes up, not after coffee

Crate training is an effective way to housebreak your puppy, and it makes the job easier for you.

and not after you watch the news to get the morning weather report. The activity around the house will wake the puppy, and as soon as he wakes up, he will have to go. If you do not take him out right away, he will use his crate as a bathroom. He will not get into the schedule you are trying to create and you will have a mess on your hands. Pick him up and take him out, let him relieve himself, remember to praise his good work and then return him to the crate. From that point on you can continue your morning activities.

Another time that it is necessary to take your puppy out is anytime after he wakes up. If you take the dog out after every nap, he will get the schedule down. He will realize that when he has to go, the place to do it is outside and not in the house. Your dog will also start to give you signs that he has to go out. These signs might be scratching at the door, grabbing his leash and bringing it to you, jumping up and down or responding to verbal cues such as, "Do you have to go outside?" or, "Want to go for a walk?" Housebreaking consists of observation and schedule. If you have a set schedule for the puppy and know what the signs are when he has to go out, you will have success in housebreaking your dog.

The crate also becomes a safe place to leave the puppy when you are not around. No one would leave a two-year-old child in a house by himself. An 8-month-old puppy is the same as a two-year-old baby. A puppy can get into trouble, chew on wires or furniture, knock things over and generally mess up your house in the

Your puppy should get used to sleeping in his crate. He will need to be taken outside right away after he wakes up.

It is important that the puppy comes to think of his crate as his "home." He will not want to soil his area by eliminating in the crate.

name of good fun. So, what would you do with a two-year-old that you wanted to keep out of trouble while your attention is diverted on other things? That's right, you might put him in a playpen. A puppy's playpen is his crate. It will just be more convenient for you and safer for the puppy to keep him in a crate when you are not watching.

If a puppy cries and barks in a crate, it is not because he is uncomfortable in the crate. He will cry just because he wants to be around the activity and people in the house. Do not think that he is suffering in the crate; just like a baby, he wants to be played with, picked up and paid attention to. Like a baby, if he is picked up and played with, the crying and barking will stop. Remember, if no one is around, he will lay quietly in the crate and go to sleep. So do not think that you are torturing your pet by putting him in a crate. You are creating a home for him and peace of mind for you.

When training a Golden for house manners, be firm and make sure the rules don't change. There are many training aids for house manners. To discourage your puppy from chewing furniture, there are products available at pet stores that you spray on the furniture. This leaves a horrible taste in the dog's mouth and he will stay away from furniture sprayed with these products. There is also a pad to place on your furniture that is similar to the electric fence in that it emits a high-pitched sound and a small shock. This pad will train your dog to stay off the furniture. There is a pad that you can put in a doorway that when touched will give a small electric shock. A puppy can be taught that the room that the doorway leads to is off limits. There are also mousetrap-like devices that keep dogs from putting their paws on the countertops. All of these products have some merit and they also all have drawbacks. Remember, though, that the best way to train a puppy is to show the dog what you want of him, tell him the command and then praise him when he completes the command successfully.

When choosing a chew toy for your dog, make sure that the toy will not break into pieces that can be swallowed.

One way to keep a puppy out of trouble when it is home alone is to have toys for him to play with. Squeaky toys, balls, stuffed animals (be careful of small parts) are all very good things for a puppy to have. Toys serve as a

Puppies are full of energy! Giving them toys to play with such as Nylafloss® will keep them busy and out of trouble.

vehicle to which puppies can release some energy. It will also keep things like furniture, shoes and clothes away from the puppy, as they will be busy chewing on the toys and not your valuables.

You should have chew toys for him. Among your choices will be pig ears, cow hooves, rawhide bones, polyurethane bones and nylon bones. The one you decide on should be the one the puppy has the most interest in. A word of caution about all chew toys, you should monitor your puppy when he is chewing on the toys. It is possible that the puppy could choke on a piece of the chew toy. The good thing about Nylabone® products and one of the reasons that they are so popular is that none of the pieces can break off and be swallowed.

CARING for a Golden Retriever

In many ways, the Golden Retriever is one of the easier breeds to care for. Besides frequent brushing, maintenance of the pet dog is relatively easy. Bathing can be done as often as you feel the need. The coat dries quickly and most dirt can be brushed out. I think a good schedule for bathing is every two months. The coat should be brushed weekly with a pin brush. When the undercoat starts to shed out, an "undercoat rake" becomes very helpful as it helps to pull out that soft undercoat.

Properly clipped nails give a dog better traction and balance. Start a weekly nail clipping routine–don't overlook this aspect of your dog's care!

Because Golden Retrievers like to swim and have floppy ears they are prone to ear infections. Checking and cleaning the ears on a weekly basis will help you prevent those infections. A good ear cleaner is a necessity with Goldens and you should have one on hand at all times.

One of the most overlooked parts of dog caring in all of dogdom is nail trimming. The nails need to be trimmed because short nails give the dog better traction on slick floors. Older dogs need their nails trimmed to give them better balance and the added traction needed to get up and move around. Start this process when you first bring home the puppy. Pick him up, touch his feet, trim his nails weekly with human nail clippers and

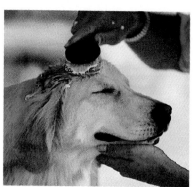

Golden Retrievers should be brushed weekly to remove dead hair and dirt from their coats.

get him used to the whole process. As he grows, purchase a good dog nail clipper and make it a habit to cut his nails every other week. There is a vein that runs down each of the nails. This vein is commonly referred to as "the quick." The more you trim the nails, the farther back into the nail the quick will recede. Thus, if you get into a routine you will never "cut the quick." If you do cut the quick, the dog will bleed. If this happens, do not rush the dog to the vet as this would only waste your time and upset your vet. Cutting the quick is analogous to a person nicking themselves shaving—neither of us will bleed to death from such an injury, it is just inconvenient. Just as with shaving, there are products that are used to stop the bleeding, such as a styptic pencil or powder that can be obtained at a pet shop. It would be wise to keep a few of them with the rest of your grooming supplies. If you find yourself without such supplies and you have cut the quick, you can use regular cooking flour or human styptic pencils to stop the bleeding.

Another area of the feet that should be taken care of are the pads. The pads are the tough, fleshy black skin on the underside of the dog's paws. The hair in the area around the pads should always be trimmed, especially in areas of the country where there is snow. If this hair is left to grow, ice balls will form in the pads. These ice balls can be painful for the dog when it comes to walking or running in below-freezing conditions.

If you have the dog out and

To prevent ice balls from forming in your dog's foot pads, keep the hair around the pads trimmed.

If your dog has been playing in a wooded area, keep an eye out for fleas, ticks, and anything else that might irritate his skin.

running in the woods or anyplace else that is not a lawn, you should check his coat and skin for ticks, burrs and other things that may cause irritations. It goes without saying that you should also keep a vigilant eye out for fleas. Remember that as long as the temperature is above freezing, fleas will survive. They can live anywhere so make sure you check your dog for fleas.

The coat of the dog tells the story of the health of your dog. A dull, lifeless coat signifies that there is something internally wrong with the dog. A coat that is falling out, is dry and feels like straw could signify a parasite infection. Monitor your dog's coat. Keep it clean, notice changes in it and it will tell you much about the overall health of your dog.

BASIC FOODS

Perhaps one of the fastest growing and most confusing

areas in the pet field is nutrition. Food A versus food B, preservatives versus natural, chicken versus lamb or soy. It can all become confusing. Read all you can about the different foods and ask questions. Find out as much as you can and then make your decision. Premium food, private label, canned, dry or moist—whatever your choice, the ultimate decision will be based on whether your dog will eat it and whether or not he will be healthy on it.

When you bring your puppy home, he should be fed what he was getting at the breeders. If this is a food that is not available in your area, ask the breeder for enough food to last until you can change over to the new food. You accomplish the change over by gradually decreasing the amount of the breeder food and replacing it with the food you will be using. The whole process should take a few days. A seven-week-old puppy should be fed three times a day and should be given a food specially formulated for puppies. You should continue to feed him three times a day for at least another month and then cut the feeding times down to two a day. If two times a day fits your lifestyle, you can continue with that schedule for the rest of his life.

How much to feed him depends on how active he is. I find that normally active adult dogs can be maintained on three cups of dog food a day; however, as activity level increases so should food intake. Also take into consideration where the dog is kept. If you have a run

Don't shove—there's plenty for everyone! A litter of hungry pups gathers around the food bowl at dinner time.

outside, in cold weather he must be fed more because he uses more calories to keep warm. In the summer you can feed him less. Food should be left down for about 20 minutes. If the dog doesn't finish it all maybe you are giving too much; cut back a little in this case. Do not leave food out at all times. The dog tends to become a

Plenty of fresh water is as important to a dog's health as a nutritious diet.

finicky eater and you will have a problem with him for his whole life.

Some dogs will stop eating when they are full and others will continue to eat as long as there is food in front of them. It is up to you to maintain your dog at the correct weight for his size. Treats can be a large portion of what you feed him in a day. Five medium dog biscuits equal one cup of kibble so be aware of how many treats your dog gets in a day. Fruits and vegetables are good alternatives to commercial treats. Try rewarding your puppy with a slice of carrot or a piece of broccoli. He will enjoy it and it is so much healthier and less fattening. If your dog responds to the fruits and vegetables, continue to introduce new fruits or vegetables to him. Add baked potatoes to his dinner or give him apples, bananas and lettuce. They are good for him and provide a source of natural vitamin C, which dogs use and absorb better than man-made vitamin C.

Watch your dog's weight. A fat dog is an unhealthy dog. Remember that dogs have relatively small bodies and five pounds overweight is considered too much. For dogs, being overweight can affect their heart, is hard on their joints and is just generally unhealthy. Keep your Golden in good weight and you will keep him fit and healthy.

With the advent of premium foods and complete diets, supplementation with vitamins has become less necessary. Vitamins taken with some of the premium foods can upset the balance of the food itself. Consult your vet or health care professional before doing a lot of supplementing.

You should always have fresh water available for your dog and I suggest a diet mainly of dry food mixed with a small amount of liquid. The choice of the food's main ingredient is up to you and your dog because he will decide what he will or won't eat. It should be some kind of meat or poultry protein; keep in mind that the first ingredient on the list of ingredients exists in the largest quantity in the food. Also know that when meat meal is listed, it could mean any kind of meat: horse, venison, even dog meat. Just as we would do for ourselves, read the labels carefully and buy a product that list a specific kind of meat and grain as its primary ingredients. Also check what it is preserved with, preferably it should be preserved naturally with Vitamin E or Vitamin C. You can, however, buy the best food with the best ingredients and if your dog doesn't eat it, the food is worth nothing, so make sure he is happy with it.

Keep Him Healthy

The Golden Retriever is a sporting dog. He is naturally active, therefore, it doesn't take much to keep him in shape. In fact, for a Golden Retriever to stay healthy and in shape it takes only a moderate amount of exercise. He makes a wonderful jogging companion, but remember to build him up gradually. A five-mile jog is not for a puppy. Start out slowly, warming him up with a brisk walk, and remember to cool him down with a trot to return his heart rate to normal. It is not necessary to jog him everyday; moderate exercises can take many forms. For the Goldens that live in cities, a walk and then some time hanging out with other dogs in the many play areas or play groups being formed is fun for the dogs and a great way for owners to meet each other.

If no play groups are available, some roughhousing in the park could be enough. A walk after every meal is essential for the city dog. Walks combined with some playtime would be adequate for the Golden.

For those who live in the suburbs, sometimes it is harder for Goldens to get adequate exercise. Remember if you work all day, some time has to be set aside to spend with your dog. A brisk ten-minute walk is necessary to get the dog mentally and physically in shape. A fenced-in backyard for the dog to run around does not necessarily mean that the dog is getting exercise. Most dogs tend to go out, relieve themselves and come back to the door. They need someone to exercise with them, play ball with them, teach them to catch a Frisbee or just walk around the backyard with them. Puppies that are left alone for a long period of time must be exercised more than the adult dog. They need time to run and play in order to release that energy they have built up. Take them out and let them run, play with them, throw a ball and wear them out so that when they come back in the house they are ready to settle down.

This Golden puppy "catches some rays" after a full day of playing and swimming in the ocean.

Golden Retrievers love the water so if you have someplace to take them swimming, by all means do it. Many people with swimming pools let the dogs swim; the only precaution you must take is to keep the dog away from the pool's lining. They can easily tear the lining with their nails. Teach dogs to climb up the pool's steps and keep them away from the lining; this should enable you to save yourself some money on pool repair. Also, chlorine tends to turn the dog's coat green and could also dry it out. To prevent this, just rinse the dog with a garden hose when he gets out of the pool. Rinsing the dog after he has been swimming in a pond might also be a good idea since the algae that is in a pond might irritate his skin.

Many people teach their Goldens to run alongside their bicycle, which is another good form of exercise. On the market is a device which hooks up to your bike and attaches to the dog so he will stay at your side. Because there is so much emphasis on human physical fitness these days, it is not difficult to find equipment that will enable the dog owner to bring his dog on a walk, run or bicycle ride. It is easy to get your dog into your exercise routine and it is great for him. If you are a person who is always putting off exercise, you will now have motivation and companionship when you finally do start to exercise. Remember that exercise is necessary for a dog to be fit, both physically and mentally.

Exercise is a necessity for dogs as well as humans. A game of fetch can provide a good release of energy for both you and your dog!

Golden Retrievers love water! The family pool may become your Golden's favorite place—make sure he can exit the pool safely, without tearing the lining.

CHOOSING A HOME WITHIN A HOME

Goldens, by their breeding and by their very nature, are people dogs. They love interacting and being with people. Given a choice, most Goldens would choose a human over another dog. It is this personality that makes them one of the most popular dogs today and the main reason why they should not be outdoor dogs. They can certainly be outside in a secure area some part of the day, but they need human interaction to be happy. Please give your Golden a lot of house time and don't relegate him to the outdoors.

When your puppy comes home, decide where you will allow the puppy to be. Most people confine the pup to the kitchen and family room, the reason being that cleaning up "accidents" in these areas is easier. As the puppy grows up, becomes housebroken and stops chewing on things you may decide to give him the run of the house. You still, however, might want to keep him out of some rooms as we all know that there are some rooms in our houses that should be dog free. As long as he is where most of the activity is, he will be happy.

You will surely be advised by the person you purchase your puppy from to "crate train" the puppy. Your question is "what is a crate?" A crate is a wire or plastic enclosure that comes in many different sizes and designs. It is a safe and convenient way to house your puppy. You can get metal crates that fold to about a suitcase size and come in different colors. You can get crates that don't fold down, crates with doors on the front or width side or doors on the long side of the crates, plastic crates that are commonly known as "airline"

Chooz® and Plaque Attackers® from Nylabone® will keep your dog occupied when he's in his crate.

crates and the newest on the market, folding airline crates. It is not "mean and cruel" but rather the most accepted and successful means of training your puppy available today. So pick your style, your color, your size and have it ready for the puppy when you bring him home. The medium size crate, about 23" W x 35" D x 26" H, is adequate for the Golden, but if you feel you would like your adult dog to have more room, by all means buy a bigger size. Remember, it will have to fit in the space you have so make sure you don't get one too big for your space. You might like to take into consideration the fact

Crates come in a variety of sizes, colors, and styles. Be sure to choose one that will accommodate your puppy as he grows into an adult.

that often times you will transport your dog in the crate in your car, which also should be thought about when you decide on a crate size. The wire variety is preferred over plastic or airline crates as it is cooler and allows the dog to see what is going on around him. Again, the best place to keep this crate is where most of the activity is in the house and where the puppy will see and be exposed to the most people. The crate will become the puppy's "safe haven," and you will find that he goes in whenever he wants to rest. After you have housebroken the dog and decide to leave the crate in the house, you will need no other bed or rug for the dog, although you might want to put a blanket or cushion in the crate. Many pet supply houses carry cushions made especially for the various sized crates.

If a crate doesn't fit into your decor, you may want to purchase a bed for your dog. There are many on the market today. I think the Golden prefers the large pillow styles. You may find your Golden wants no part of a bed but prefers to sleep on a rug. Each dog is an individual and will definitely let you know what his choice of sleeping arrangements will be. In the summertime you will find your dog in the coolest place in the house—tile floors, air conditioned rooms, even bathtubs.

OUTDOOR ARRANGEMENTS

A fenced-in backyard is a safe and secure enclosure for your dog. You can train him to use one spot in the yard for a toilet area by always taking him to that one place. He will soon learn that that is the place to go to the bathroom.

Be mindful of the plants that are in your backyard as many common plants can be poisonous to your puppy. Some of the plants to look out for are pokeweed, foxglove and yew. A puppy likes to run and play and chew and dig. If you are a person who takes

Your Golden may prefer sleeping in a bed to sleeping in his crate.

great pride in your yard, stay outside with your puppy to make sure he understands what he can and cannot do. Remember the two rules of obedience—firmness and consistency. Do not yell at him *after* he has dug up your prize plants; rather, stop him before he digs them out.

Another idea might be to build a run, which is a chain-link enclosure that will confine the dog to a certain place in the yard as well as protect your yard. Certainly, if someone is out in the yard, let the puppy out. However, if no one is outside, it protects the puppy and your yard. It is also an excellent solution to the person without a fenced-in backyard. The run should go somewhere where the puppy or adult dog will be safe and where he can be outside in nice weather. It is also a nice alternative to the nighttime walk when it is raining or cold. It should be at least 5 feet tall, with 6 feet

In hot summer weather, your dog will often seek out the coolest places in the house, such as rooms with air conditioning or tile floors.

being ideal. The perimeter should be made of railroad ties with at least two of the ties buried in the ground, as the dog will sometimes try to dig his way out. The chain-link would be set on top of the ties. I prefer the 1-inch chain-link as the dogs are less likely to get anything caught in it. It is also less likely that they can chew through it. If you are wondering, yes, they can chew through chain-link fencing. The run should be placed where it will be shaded during the hottest time of the day but where it also could get some sun on colder days.

If you leave the ground grass-covered, you will have mud in a couple of weeks. A good source of ground cover is pea gravel. Another ground cover is cement, which is easy to clean and disinfect. The down side of cement is that it is harder on dogs' feet and has a tendency to break their coats.

Inside the run you should provide a raised platform for your dog to get off the ground, and a dog house is always welcome. There are many different kinds on the market, plastic or wood, or you could make your own. The dog house should be big enough for your dog to turn around in. It should have a raised floor and a flap over the door to protect from the weather.

You should always provide fresh water for your pet in the run. Remember that he is basically a house pet and should not be left out in extreme weather conditions.

I would like to say a few words about another form of confinement. It is the tie-out, cable or chain. This is definitely not a good method of confining your dog; the risks are too great. Your dog can choke himself on the chain. He has no way to escape from anything that comes into the yard, like a rabid raccoon. If there are children in your neighborhood, they could come and tease him. If he starts jumping and lunging for them, all of a sudden you could have a vicious Golden on your hands. The whole method puts your dog at the mercy of a chain and it is not a good idea.

Another form of enclosure that is relatively new on the market is electric fencing. No, this is not the type of fence that emits a 100,000 volt charge to anything unfortunate enough to touch it. Electric fences are wires dug into or laid on the ground around a certain perimeter. It is electrified and your dog wears a special collar that has a receiver on it. There is a training period where the dog is startled by a loud noise when it goes near the wire and followed up by a mild shock when it gets close to the fencing. It is an excellent way to keep dogs from flower beds, swimming pools or the street. If you have a very stubborn dog, the shock may not be enough and the system will be ineffective. The one draw back to this procedure is that even though it may keep your pet in, it does nothing to keep other dogs or animals out.

HOUSEKEEPING

Whatever you decide on or wherever you decide to keep your pet, make sure that all the areas are kept clean. Blankets and beds should be washed regularly. Food and water dishes should be washed daily, crates should be scrubbed and dog houses should be cleaned and hosed down. All environments must be kept free of parasites, especially fleas which carry disease. There are cleaning products especially used to get rid of these parasites. One of the best disinfectants is household bleach. Used in various concentrations, it kills almost any form of bacteria, most parasites and even fleas.

Feces should be picked up and disposed of at least once a day. If you leave it out, it draws flies, gets stepped on and becomes a health hazard for your dog. If you choose a run and put pea gravel down, sprinkle it with bleach and hose it down weekly, this will control odor and parasites. Remember, your dog's physical and emotional well being are closely related. The Golden Retriever

Your dog's crate is his special area—be sure to keep it, along with his other accessories, clean and parasite-free.

who is well fed, groomed, exercised and whose environment is clean is a happy dog.

IDENTIFYING YOUR DOG

You will always want to keep your dog safe and confined to his space. Sometimes, however, no matter how much care we take, accidents happen and our dog escapes, runs away or, worse, is

There are many modern methods of identification available to dog owners. A recent picture of your dog can be helpful if he should get lost.

stolen. Today there are many ways of identifying your dog. While it will not assure you that your dog will be returned to you, it will help in locating and positively identifying your pet. You can have your pet tattooed, usually on the inside rear thigh, with any number you wish: A.K.C. registration number, your social security number or your lucky number. That number is then registered with a national clearing house. If your dog is found, whoever finds him can call and find out who he belongs to. Another method that is gaining popularity is the "microchip." A microchip is implanted in the puppy in the neck area. The chip has an identifying number that is registered to you. The dog can be scanned, much like the supermarkets scan your groceries, and then you can be notified as to where your dog has been found. Also keep a recent picture of your dog handy so you can put out flyers locally if your dog should get lost. We hope our dogs never get lost but these are good precautions that we can take to help us find them if the unthinkable does happen.

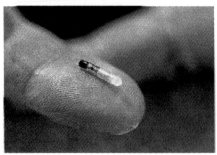

The newest method of identification is microchipping. The microchip is a computer chip that is no bigger than a grain of rice.

BREEDING Your Golden Retriever

If you decide that spaying or neutering is not an option for your pet because you intend to breed your female or use your male as a stud, remember that you as a breeder are under the same obligations to the breed as previous Golden Retriever breeders. The obligations include the presence of all the aforementioned clearances (eyes, hip and heart) in your breeding stock. You must also have plenty of time to spend with a litter of puppies. You will have to spend time with the puppies and the people who will come to your home to look and maybe even buy your Goldens. Above all though, your dog should

If you intend to breed your Golden Retriever, be aware of the responsibilities and obligations you have to the breed.

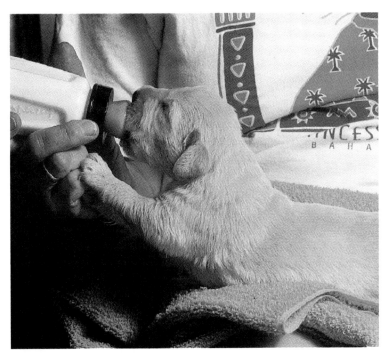

Properly caring for a litter of puppies can be an expensive and time-consuming endeavor.

be a good representative of the breed. He should be able to pass on all the wonderful attributes that make the Golden Retriever so special.

Breeding is not a simple or inexpensive undertaking. The expenses alone could be very high. Remember that you have to get clearances and you have to pay for a stud. After the puppies are born, there should be veterinary appointments for both the mother and puppies. Taking care of the puppies properly easily could run you a month's salary. You could also spend all that money and have nothing to show for it if the breeding doesn't take or something happens to the mother or the puppies or both.

Breeding your dog can be a wonderful learning experience and a rewarding project to undertake, but you must remember that there are dangers in breeding your pet. All dogs that enter a breeding program must have a hip clearance. Most of the time the test involved in a hip clearance requires the dog to be put under anesthesia. This presents a danger in that your pet maybe allergic to anesthesia, which could result in death.

We must also remember, as with any species, it is more dangerous to be pregnant than not and dogs are no exception. There is always the possibility of losing your bitch during whelping (giving birth). If the mother does die during whelping, you will have to hand-raise her puppies. This means feeding puppies every four hours around the clock, stimulating them to move their bowels and emptying their kidneys, burping them, keeping them warm and trying to give them

If a pregnant dog should die while giving birth, it is the breeder's responsibility to become the litter's "surrogate mother."

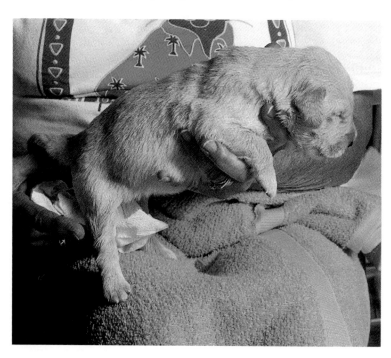

the nurturing and comfort that their mother would have given them.

You must also consider that not all puppies are born healthy and sometimes we must make decisions as to whether or not a puppy should be put down. As everyone knows, it is very hard to see a young puppy die.

When you are deciding whether or not to spay your pet, keep in mind that there is the possibility of losing her if she becomes pregnant. You must decide if you want to take the chance and risk losing your beloved pet. If it is important to have another dog, consider buying one. If you want to breed because you think it would be a good experience for the kids, remember that there are good tapes around on dog birthing. If it is just to have puppies, keep in mind that there are thousands of puppies abandoned or put to sleep every year because there are no homes for them. In the end the final decision will be yours; just remember that you take the chance of losing your pet in order to have the litter of puppies.

Raising a litter of puppies can be a rewarding experience, but there are many consequences to consider before deciding to breed your Golden Retriever.

If you decide to use your male as a stud dog, you will need to get clearances. Remember the dangers of x-rays and anesthesia. You may also see some territorial tendencies in your stud dog. He could become more aggressive toward other males and will have a greater tendency to mark. Many times when habits are formed, neutering later in the dog's life will not take them away. Think carefully of using your male or female for breeding and consider all the consequences. Most of the time spaying or neutering is the right choice for your pet.

TRAINING Your Golden Retriever

An 8-week-old Golden Retriever can be taught many things. He can be taught to wait at the door, have his feet wiped off, fetch a ball, not jump up on people and sit and stay. A puppy's attention span, though, is very short so training lessons should not last more than five minutes. Anything more than that might be counterproductive, as the puppy will try to focus his attention on something else.

The Golden Retriever responds best to firmness and consistency. To train your Golden to sit, give him the command sit, show him what sit is and then praise him when he obeys your command. This is usually enough for the young puppy to understand what is wanted of him. Remember, Golden Retrievers love to please so usually no harsh commands or sharp corrections are needed for your puppy. Firmness, consistency and praise are the keys to correct training procedures.

There are many avenues of training available for your pet today. Private training, group training, puppy kindergarten and competition are all excellent ways for your dog to receive not only obedience training but socialization experience. The Golden loves to be active

Always be consistent with your gestures and commands. While the dog is "down," the trainer gives a hand signal and verbal command for "stay."

with his mind and body. Puppy kindergarten can provide that kind of stimulation by helping him develop his early social skills along with his learning of simple obedience commands. Group training continues his social skills training while progressing to more complicated obedience commands. Competition training trains you and your dog to compete in obedience trials. Private training often times works more with specific problems than with simple obedience or housebreaking.

Always give your dog praise when he obeys your command. This will reinforce what is expected of him—Golden Retrievers love to please their owners!

Start training your dog with basic commands such as "sit" and "stay."

Each trainer will have their own

These Golden Retrievers, pictured here with their owner Nona Kilgore Bauer, are practicing retrieving.

method of training and all methods do not work with all dogs. With your Golden, I think you should find someone that uses the praise type of training rather than a harsh correction method. Most Goldens will respond to a show me, tell me, praise me type of training. Just because Goldens are easy going, friendly dogs, do not make the mistake of thinking your dog doesn't need any kind of training. Every dog needs training to make both of your lives easier, and Goldens are no exception. I do think that all Goldens need some sort of training and I do like the group training because it provides socialization for you and the puppy.

SPECIAL REQUIREMENTS OF THE SPORTING DOG

The Golden Retriever was bred for hunting and should you decide that you would like to hunt with your dog, keep a few simple things in mind. Early retrieving should be fun. Using three training dummies, throw them short distances and in patterns so that the puppy can get used to watching where they fall. Then give him directions as to how to pick up the dummies. Once he has the dummy, teach him to bring it back to you. Within four to five months of consistent practice, you will have a puppy confident enough to retrieve dummies from 40 or 50 feet away.

You will eventually want to introduce your puppy to a real bird. This is usually done by allowing the puppy to retrieve a duck or pheasant wing. However, you don't want to use that for a long period of time because the pup or adult dog will be trained to pick up the whole bird by the wing. It is better to use a small

If you want to hunt with your Golden, he must be able to retrieve in water. Here, Ch. Laurell's Jiminy Crickett, owned by the author, practices water retrieving.

dead pigeon or duck to get your young dog used to birds.

While Golden Retrievers love water, their introduction to it should be fun, using an area where the puppy may walk or wade in the shallow water. If you push him into the cold water, he may develop a dislike for it and never do it again. This could be a problem for you if you want the dog to perform water retrieving. It helps if you can have older dogs to play with the pup in the water. Start water retrieving in a place where the puppy is still able to wade into the water and where his feet still touch the bottom of the pond, river or lake. Throw the dummy into the water at a distance that allows the puppy to wade into the water. When you want to train the puppy to retrieve from farther distances, bring in an adult dog to retrieve the dummy. Throw the dummy for the adult dog and when the adult dog swims out to get it, the puppy should follow.

These are the very basic principles of hunting. You must form a relationship with your hunting dog and you must repeat and repeat your training so he knows what is expected of him.

Whether you are training your Golden to be a hunting companion or a field competitor, remember to keep his training consistent and fun.

For the puppy there are three things to keep in mind: be consistent, keep it simple and make it fun. If you follow these three suggestions, you will have a good hunter and a great companion.

If you want to know more about hunting and training, there are clubs devoted exclusively to hunting and competitive field trials in most areas of the country. You should become involved with them.

ADAPTABILITY

Lord Tweedmouth's selective breeding and the very foundations of the Golden Retriever ensured us of a breed that could adapt to many different situations. The Golden was selectively bred to become a true retriever. This true retriever attribute coupled with the best

After a few months of training with practice dummies, your dog will be ready to practice retrieving birds. This Golden Retriever is owned by Nona Kilgore Bauer.

characteristics of hunting dogs make the Golden a very adaptable dog. It is false that the city is unsuitable for a Golden; it false that the country is unsuitable for the Golden, or the cold, or the hot or the snow. The Golden Retriever seems to adjust to any situation and any place that we put him. He seems to sense what is expected of him and perform the tasks that are given to him. We see this often in Golden rescues when 10- or 11-year-old dogs become available for adoption. They go to their new home after ten years of a previous home and previous owners and

The Golden Retriever's ability to learn quickly and desire to please his owner make him a top obedience dog and a loyal companion.

we still get glowing reports on how well they have adjusted to the new lifestyle. It's almost as if they had lived their whole lives in their new homes.

Golden Retrievers like to please. They like to be in your good graces and will do almost anything to be true. In their willingness to please, they can be trained easily. The joke among Golden breeders is that they are born with a CD. While this is not exactly true, they do seem to be very intelligent; this intelligence coupled with the intense desire to please make for a dog that is very accommodating.

Golden Retrievers have quick minds and seem to catch onto things very fast. In watching Goldens, they almost seem to watch the world and observe what is going on around them. They do not have the intensity of some of the other breeds that are out there and I am sure they do not have the raw intelligence that other breeds might have, but Goldens seem to learn faster and easier than most.

Many of the top obedience dogs are Goldens, which doesn't necessarily prove that they are the smartest dogs. It does, however, illustrate the intense desire to please found in all Goldens. This desire makes them appear very smart. Intelligent or not, they are very easy to train and are used in many different ways in the world today.

SPORT of Purebred Dogs

Welcome to the exciting and sometimes frustrating sport of dogs. No doubt you are trying to learn more about dogs or you wouldn't be deep into this book. This section covers the basics that may entice you, further your knowledge and help you to understand the dog world. If you decide to give showing, obedience or any other dog activities a try, then I suggest you seek further help from the appropriate source.

Dog showing has been a very popular sport for a long time and has been taken quite seriously by some. Others only enjoy it as a hobby.

The Kennel Club in England was formed in 1859, the American Kennel Club was established in 1884 and the Canadian Kennel Club was formed in 1888. The purpose of these clubs was to register purebred dogs and maintain their Stud Books. In the beginning, the concept of registering dogs was not readily accepted. More than 36 million dogs have been enrolled in the AKC Stud Book since its inception in 1888. Presently the kennel clubs not only register dogs but adopt and enforce rules and regulations governing dog shows, obedience trials and field trials. Over the years they have fostered and encouraged interest in the health and welfare of the purebred dog. They routinely donate funds to veterinary research for study on genetic disorders.

Following are the addresses of the kennel clubs in the United States, Great Britain and Canada.

Handlers "gait" their Goldens in a conformation show. Gaiting enables the judge to see the dogs in motion.

The American Kennel Club
51 Madison Avenue
New York, NY 10010
(Their registry is located at: 5580
Centerview Drive, STE 200,
Raleigh, NC 27606-3390)

The Kennel Club
1 Clarges Street
Piccadilly, London, WIY 8AB,
England

The broad jump is one of the exercises in an obedience competition.

The Canadian Kennel Club
111 Eglinton Avenue
East Toronto, Ontario M6S 4V7
Canada

This Golden competes in agility, a competition which can be described as an obstacle course for dogs.

Today there are numerous activities that are enjoyable for both the dog and the handler.

Some of the activities include conformation showing, obedience competition, tracking, agility, the Canine Good Citizen Certificate, and a wide range of instinct tests that vary from breed to breed. Where you start depends upon your goals which early on may not be readily apparent.

Puppy Kindergarten

Every puppy will benefit from this class. PKT is the foundation for all future dog activities from conformation to "couch potatoes." Pet owners should make an effort to attend even if they never expect to show their dog. The class is designed for puppies about three months of age with graduation at approximately five months of age. All the puppies will be in the same age group and, even though some may be a little unruly, there should not be any real problem. This class will teach the puppy some beginning obedience. As in all obedience classes the owner learns how to train his own dog. The PKT class gives the puppy the opportunity to interact with other puppies in the same age group and

Use your dog's name when giving him a command and reward him with praise or a treat. Here, the trainer demonstrates the command "sit."

exposes him to strangers, which is very important. Some dogs grow up with behavior problems, one of them being fear of strangers. As you can see, there can be much to gain from this class.

There are some basic obedience exercises that every dog should learn. Some of these can be started with puppy kindergarten.

Sit

One way of teaching the sit is to have your dog on your left side with the leash in your right hand, close to the collar. Pull up on the leash and at the same time reach around his hindlegs with your left hand and tuck them in. As you are doing this say, "Beau, sit." Always use the dog's name when you give an active command. Some owners like to use a treat holding it over the dog's head. The dog will need to sit to get the treat. Encourage the dog to hold the sit for a few seconds, which will

The command "down" can be taught by having your dog sit and using your hands to move his forelegs into the "down" position.

eventually be the beginning of the Sit/Stay. Depending on how cooperative he is, you can rub him under the chin or stroke his back. It is a good time to establish eye contact.

Down

Sit the dog on your left side and kneel down beside him with the leash in your right hand. Reach over him with your left hand and grasp his left foreleg. With your right hand, take his right foreleg and pull his legs forward while you say, "Beau, down." If he tries to get up, lean on his shoulder to encourage him to stay down. It will relax your dog if you stroke his back while he is down. Try to encourage him to stay down for a few seconds as preparation for the Down/Stay.

Heel

The definition of heeling is the dog walking under control at your left heel. Your puppy will learn controlled walking in the puppy kindergarten class, which will eventually lead to heeling. The command is "Beau, heel," and you start off briskly with your left foot. Your leash is in your right hand and your left hand is holding it about half way down. Your left hand should be able to control the leash and there should be a little slack in it. You want him to walk with you with your leg somewhere between his nose and his shoulder. You need to encourage him to stay with you, not forging (in front of you) or lagging behind you. It is best to keep him on a fairly short lead. Do not allow the lead to become tight. It is far better to give him a little jerk when necessary and remind him to heel. When you come to a halt, be prepared physically to make him sit. It takes practice to become coordinated. There are excellent books on training that you may wish to purchase. Your instructor should be able to recommend one for you.

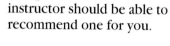

"Heel" is another important basic command. Your dog should learn to walk at your heel at a controlled pace.

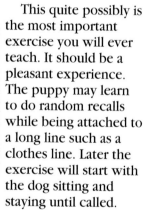

Recall

This quite possibly is the most important exercise you will ever teach. It should be a pleasant experience. The puppy may learn to do random recalls while being attached to a long line such as a clothes line. Later the exercise will start with the dog sitting and staying until called. The command is "Beau, come." Let your command be happy. You want your dog to come willingly and faithfully. The recall could save his life if he sneaks out the door. In practicing the recall, let him jump on you or touch you before you reach for him. If he is shy, then kneel down to his level. Reaching for the insecure dog could frighten him, and he may not be willing to come again in the future. Lots of praise and a treat would be in order whenever you do a recall. Under no circumstances should you ever correct your dog when he has come to you. Later in formal obedience your dog will be required to sit in front of you after recalling and then go to heel position.

In conformation showing, a dog is judged based on his appearance and on how well he conforms to the standard of his breed.

CONFORMATION

Conformation showing is our oldest dog show sport. This type of showing is based on the dog's appearance—that is his structure, movement and attitude. When considering this type of showing, you need to be aware of your breed's standard and be able to evaluate your dog compared to that standard. The breeder of your puppy or other experienced breeders would be good sources for such an evaluation. Puppies can go through lots of changes over a period of time. I always say most puppies start out as promising hopefuls and then after maturing may be disappointing as show candidates. Even so this should not deter them from being excellent pets.

Usually conformation training classes are offered by the local kennel or obedience clubs. These are excellent places for training puppies. The puppy should be able to walk on a lead before entering such a class. Proper ring procedure and technique for posing (stacking) the dog will be demonstrated as well as gaiting the dog. Usually certain patterns are used in the ring such as the triangle or the "L." Conformation class, like the PKT class, will give your youngster the opportunity to socialize with different breeds of dogs and humans too.

It takes some time to learn the routine of conformation showing. Usually one starts at the puppy matches which may be AKC Sanctioned or Fun Matches. These matches are generally for puppies from two or three months to a year old, and there may be classes for the adult over the age of 12 months. Similar to point shows, the classes are divided by sex and after completion of the classes in that breed or variety, the class winners compete for Best of Breed or Variety. The winner goes on to compete in the Group and the Group winners compete for Best in

It will take your dog some time to get used to being in the show ring and to being handled by the judges.

Conformation winners, like this Golden Retriever, exemplify all aspects of their breed's standard.

Match. No championship points are awarded for match wins.

A few matches can be great training for puppies even though there is no intention to go on showing. Matches enable the puppy to meet new people and be handled by a stranger—the judge. It is also a change of environment, which broadens the horizon for both dog and handler. Matches and other dog activities boost the confidence of the handler and especially the younger handlers.

Earning an AKC championship is built on a point system, which is different from Great Britain. To become an AKC Champion of Record the dog must earn 15 points. The number of points earned each time depends upon the number of dogs in competition. The number of points available at each show depends upon the breed, its sex and the location of the show. The United States is divided into ten AKC zones. Each zone has its own set of points. The purpose of the zones is to try to equalize the points available from breed to breed and area to area.The AKC adjusts the point scale annually.

The number of points that can be won at a show are between one and five. Three-, four- and five-point wins are considered majors. Not only does the dog need 15 points won under three different judges, but those points must include two majors under two different judges. Canada also works on a point system but majors are not required.

Dogs always show before bitches. The classes available to those seeking points are: Puppy (which may be divided into 6 to 9 months and 9 to 12 months); 12 to 18 months; Novice; Bred-by-Exhibitor; American-bred; and Open. The class winners of the same sex of each breed or variety compete against each other for Winners Dog and Winners Bitch. A Reserve Winners Dog and Reserve Winners Bitch are also awarded but do not carry any points unless the Winners win is disallowed by AKC. The Winners Dog and Bitch compete with the specials (those dogs that have attained championship) for Best of Breed or Variety, Best of Winners and Best of Opposite Sex. It is possible to pick up an extra point or even a major if the points are higher for the defeated winner than those of Best of Winners. The latter would get the higher total from the defeated winner.

At an all-breed show, each Best of Breed or Variety winner will go on to his respective Group and then the Group winners will compete against each other for Best in Show. There are seven Groups: Sporting, Hounds, Working, Terriers, Toys, Non-Sporting and Herding. Obviously there are no Groups at specialty shows (those shows that have only one breed or a show such as the American Spaniel Club's Flushing Spaniel Show, which is for all flushing spaniel breeds).

Earning a championship in England is somewhat different since they do not have a point system. Challenge Certificates

are awarded if the judge feels the dog is deserving regardless of the number of dogs in competition. A dog must earn three Challenge Certificates under three different judges,

This Golden Retriever is carefully examined by a conformation judge.

Showing your puppy will build his confidence in the ring. This is Goldenbear's Yahoo Crazy, owned by James and Cindy Lichtenberger, winning a puppy match.

with at least one of these Certificates being won after the age of 12 months. Competition is very strong and entries may be higher than they are in the U.S. The Kennel Club's Challenge Certificates are only available at Championship Shows.

In England, The Kennel Club regulations require that certain dogs, Border Collies and Gundog breeds, qualify in a working capacity (i.e., obedience or field trials) before becoming a full Champion. If they do not qualify in the working aspect, then they are designated a Show Champion, which is equivalent to the AKC's Champion of Record. A Gundog may be granted the title of Field Trial Champion (FT Ch.) if it passes all the tests in the field but would also have to qualify in conformation before becoming a full Champion. A Border Collie that earns the title of Obedience Champion (Ob Ch.) must also qualify in the conformation ring before becoming a Champion.

The U.S. doesn't have a designation full Champion but does award for Dual and Triple Champions. The Dual Champion must be a Champion of Record, and either Champion Tracker, Herding Champion, Obedience Trial Champion or Field Champion. Any dog that has been awarded the titles of Champion of Record, and any two of the following: Champion Tracker, Herding Champion, Obedience Trial Champion or Field Champion, may be designated as a Triple Champion.

The shows in England seem to put more emphasis on breeder judges than those in the U.S. There is much competition within the breeds. Therefore the quality of the individual breeds should be very good. In the United States we tend to have more "all around judges" (those that judge multiple breeds) and use the breeder judges at the specialty shows. Breeder judges are more familiar with their own breed since they are actively breeding that breed or did so at one time. Americans emphasize Group and Best in Show wins and promote them accordingly.

This Golden Retriever, pictured with Ray Laureano, relaxes in the shade after winning a show ribbon.

It is my understanding that the shows in England can be very large and extend over several days, with the Groups being scheduled on different days. I believe there is only one all-breed show in the U.S. that extends over two days, the Westminster Kennel Club Show. In our country we have cluster shows, where several different clubs will use the same show site over consecutive days.

Westminster Kennel Club is our most prestigious show although the entry is limited to 2500. In recent years, entry has been limited to Champions. This show is more formal than the majority of the shows with the judges wearing formal attire and the handlers fashionably dressed. In most instances the quality of the dogs is superb. After all, it is a show of Champions. It is a good show to study the AKC registered breeds and is by far the most exciting—especially since it is televised! WKC is one of the few shows in this country that is still benched. This means the dog must be in his benched area during the show hours except when he is being groomed, in the ring, or being exercised.

Gaiting is the part of the conformation show in which the dog's movement is judged. Goldens should exhibit easy movement with good front leg extension.

Typically, the handlers are very particular about their appearances. They are careful not to wear something that will detract from their dog but will perhaps enhance it. American ring procedure is quite formal compared to that of other countries. I remember being reprimanded by a judge because I made a suggestion to a friend holding my second dog outside the ring. I certainly could have used more discretion so I would not call attention to myself. There is a certain etiquette expected between the judge and exhibitor and among the other exhibitors. Of course it is not always the case but the judge is supposed to be polite, not engaging in small talk or even acknowledging that he knows the handler. I understand that there is a more informal and relaxed atmosphere at the shows in other countries. For instance, the dress code is more casual. I can see where this might be more fun for the exhibitor and especially for the novice. This country is very handler-oriented in many of the breeds. It is true, in most instances, that the experienced professional handler can present the dog better and will have a feel for what a judge likes.

In England, Crufts is The Kennel Club's own show and is most assuredly the largest dog show in the world. They've been known to have an entry of nearly 20,000, and the show lasts four days. Entry is only gained by qualifying through winning in specified classes at another Championship Show. Westminster is strictly conformation, but Crufts exhibitors and spectators enjoy not only conformation but obedience, agility and a multitude of exhibitions as well. Obedience was admitted in 1957 and agility in 1983.

If you are handling your own dog, please give some consideration to your apparel. For sure the dress code at matches is more informal than the point shows. However, you should wear something a little more appropriate than beach attire or ragged jeans and bare feet. If you check out the handlers and see what is presently fashionable, you'll catch on. Men usually dress with a shirt and tie and a nice sports coat. Whether you are male or female, you will want to wear comfortable clothes and shoes. You need

Remember to bring any necessary grooming equipment to the show with you. Your dog will need a pre-show "touch-up" like the Golden pictured here.

to be able to run with your dog and you certainly don't want to take a chance of falling and hurting yourself. Heaven forbid, if nothing else, you'll upset your dog. Women usually wear a dress or two-piece outfit, preferably with pockets to carry bait, comb, brush, etc. In this case men are the lucky ones with all their pockets. Ladies, think about where your dress will be if

In Junior Handling, the handler is judged solely on his or her ability to exhibit and present the dog. you need to kneel on the floor and also think about running. Does it allow freedom to do so?

Years ago, after toting around all the baby paraphernalia, I found toting the dog and necessities a breeze. You need to take along dog; crate; ex pen (if you use one); extra newspaper; water pail and water; all required grooming equipment, including hair dryer and extension cord; table; chair for you; bait for dog and lunch for you and friends; and, last but not least, clean up materials, such as plastic bags, paper towels, and perhaps a bath towel and some shampoo—just in case. Don't forget your entry confirmation and directions to the show.

If you are showing in obedience, then you will want to wear pants. Many of our top obedience handlers wear pants that are color-coordinated with their dogs. The philosophy is that imperfections in the black dog will be less obvious next to your black pants.

Whether you are showing in conformation, Junior Showmanship or obedience, you need to watch the clock and be sure you are not late. It is customary to pick up your conformation armband a few minutes before the start of the class. They will not wait for you and if you are on the show grounds and not in the ring, you will upset everyone. It's a little more complicated picking up your obedience armband if you show later in the class. If you have not picked up your armband and they get to your number, you may not be allowed to show. It's best to pick up your armband early, but then you may show earlier than expected if other handlers don't pick up. Customarily all conflicts should be discussed with the judge prior to the start of the class.

Junior Showmanship

The Junior Showmanship Class is a wonderful way to build self confidence even if there are no aspirations of staying with the dog-show game later in life. Frequently, Junior Showmanship becomes the background of those who become successful exhibitors/handlers in the future. In some instances it is taken

Although conformation is not judged in Junior Handling, a well-groomed dog in good condition is a positive reflection on the young handler.

Junior Handling is a wonderful way for a young person to build confidence and a strong foundation for future showing and handling.

very seriously, and success is measured in terms of wins. The Junior Handler is judged solely on his ability and skill in presenting his dog. The dog's conformation is not to be considered by the judge. Even so the condition and grooming of the dog may be a reflection upon the handler.

Usually the matches and point shows include different classes. The Junior Handler's dog may be entered in a breed or obedience class and even shown by another person in that class. Junior Showmanship classes are usually divided by age and perhaps sex. The age is determined by the handler's age on the day of the show. The classes are:

Novice Junior for those at least ten and under 14 years of age who at time of entry closing have not won three first places in a Novice Class at a licensed or member show.

Novice Senior for those at least 14 and under 18 years of age who at the time of entry closing have not won three first places in a Novice Class at a licensed or member show.

Open Junior for those at least ten and under 14 years of age who at the time of entry closing have won at least three first places in a Novice Junior Showmanship Class at a licensed or member show with competition present.

Open Senior for those at least 14 and under 18 years of age who at time of entry closing have won at least three first places in a Novice Junior Showmanship Class at a licensed or member show with competition present.

Junior Handlers must include their AKC Junior Handler number on each show entry. This needs to be obtained from the AKC.

CANINE GOOD CITIZEN

The AKC sponsors a program to encourage dog owners to train their dogs. Local clubs perform the pass/fail tests, and dogs who pass are awarded a Canine Good Citizen Certificate. Proof of vaccination is required at the time of participation. The test includes:

1. Accepting a friendly stranger.
2. Sitting politely for petting.
3. Appearance and grooming.
4. Walking on a loose leash.
5. Walking through a crowd.
6. Sit and down on command/staying in place.
7. Come when called.
8. Reaction to another dog.
9. Reactions to distractions.
10. Supervised separation.

If more effort was made by pet owners to accomplish these exercises, fewer dogs would be cast off to the humane shelter.

A Golden Retriever participates in the Canine Good Citizen Test, which is sponsored by the AKC to encourage owners to train their dogs.

This Golden demonstrates retrieving over the high jump.

OBEDIENCE

Obedience is necessary, without a doubt, but it can also become a wonderful hobby or even an obsession. In my opinion, obedience classes and competition can provide wonderful companionship, not only with your dog but with your classmates or fellow competitors. It is always gratifying to discuss your dog's problems with others who have had similar experiences. The AKC acknowledged Obedience around 1936, and it has changed tremendously even though many of the exercises are basically the same. Today, obedience competition is just that—very competitive. Even so, it is possible for every obedience exhibitor to come home a winner (by earning qualifying scores) even though he/she may not earn a placement in the class.

Most of the obedience titles are awarded after earning three qualifying scores (legs) in the appropriate class under three different judges. These classes offer a perfect score of 200, which is extremely rare. Each of the class exercises has its own point value. A leg is earned after receiving a score of at least 170 and at least 50 percent of the points available in each exercise. The titles are:

Companion Dog–CD
This is called the Novice Class and the exercises are:

1. Heel on leash and figure 8	40 points
2. Stand for examination	30 points
3. Heel free	40 points
4. Recall	30 points
5. Long sit–one minute	30 points
6. Long down–three minutes	30 points
Maximum total score	200 points

Companion Dog Excellent–CDX
This is the Open Class and the exercises are:

1. Heel off leash and figure 8	40 points
2. Drop on recall	30 points
3. Retrieve on flat	20 points
4. Retrieve over high jump	30 points
5. Broad jump	20 points
6. Long sit–three minutes (out of sight)	30 points
7. Long down–five minutes (out of sight)	30 points
Maximum total score	200 points

Utility Dog–UD
The Utility Class exercises are:

1. Signal Exercise	40 points
2. Scent discrimination-Article 1	30 points
3. Scent discrimination-Article 2	30 points
4. Directed retrieve	30 points
5. Moving stand and examination	30 points
6. Directed jumping	40 points
Maximum total score	200 points

After achieving the UD title, you may feel inclined to go after the UDX and/or OTCh. The

This Golden is heeling in an obedience competition.

UDX (Utility Dog Excellent) title went into effect in January 1994. It is not easily attained. The title requires qualifying simultaneously ten times in Open B and Utility B but not necessarily at consecutive shows.

A Golden Retriever prepares to go over the high jump.

The OTCh (Obedience Trial Champion) is awarded after the dog has earned his UD and then goes on to earn 100 championship points, a first place in Utility, a first place in Open and another first place in either class. The placements must be won under three different judges at all-breed obedience trials. The points are determined by the number of dogs competing in the Open B and Utility B classes. The OTCh title precedes the dog's name.

Obedience matches (AKC Sanctioned, Fun, and Show and Go) are usually available. Usually they are sponsored by the local obedience clubs. When preparing an obedience dog for a title, you will find matches very helpful. Fun Matches and Show and Go Matches are more lenient in allowing you to make corrections in the ring. I frequently train (correct) in the ring and inform the judge that I would like to do so and to please mark me "exhibition." This means that I will not be eligible for any prize. This type of training is usually very necessary for the Open and Utility Classes. AKC Sanctioned Obedience Matches do not allow corrections in the ring since they must abide by the AKC Obedience Regulations. If you are interested in showing in obedience, then you should contact the AKC for a copy of the Obedience Regulations.

TRACKING

Tracking is officially classified obedience, but I feel it should have its own category. There are three tracking titles available: Tracking Dog (TD), Tracking Dog Excellent (TDX), Variable Surface Tracking (VST). If all three tracking titles are obtained, then the dog officially becomes a CT (Champion Tracker). The CT will go in front of the dog's name.

A TD may be earned anytime and does not have to follow the other obedience titles. There are many exhibitors that prefer tracking to obedience, and there are others like myself that do both. In my experience with small dogs, I prefer to earn the CD and CDX before attempting tracking. My reasoning is that small dogs are closer to the mat in the obedience rings and therefore it's too easy to put the nose down and sniff. Tracking encourages sniffing. Of course this depends on the dog. I've had some dogs that tracked around the ring and others (TDXs) who wouldn't think of sniffing in the ring.

Tracking Dog–TD

A dog must be certified by an AKC tracking judge that he is ready to perform in an AKC test. The AKC can provide the names of tracking judges in your area that you can contact for certification. Depending on where you live, you may have to travel a distance if there is no local tracking judge. The certification track will be equivalent to a regular AKC track. A regulation track must be 440 to 500 yards long with at least two right-angle turns out in the open. The track will be aged 30 minutes to two hours. The handler has two starting flags at the beginning of the track to indicate the direction started. The dog works on a harness and 40-foot lead and must work at least 20 feet in front of the handler. An article (either a dark glove or wallet) will be dropped at the end of the track, and the dog must indicate it but not necessarily retrieve it.

People always ask me what the dog tracks. In my opinion, initially, the beginner on the short-aged track tracks the tracklayer. Eventually the dog learns to track the disturbed vegetation and learns to differentiate between tracks. Getting started with tracking requires reading the AKC regulations and a good book on tracking plus finding other tracking enthusiasts. I like to work on the buddy system. That is—we lay tracks for each other so we can practice blind tracks. It is possible to train on your own, but if you are a beginner, it is a lot more entertaining to track with a buddy. Tracking is my favorite dog sport. It's rewarding seeing the dog use his natural ability.

Tracking Dog Excellent–TDX

The TDX track is 800 to 1000 yards long and is aged three to five hours. There will be five to seven turns. An article is left at the starting flag, and three other articles must be indicated on the track. There is only one flag at the start, so it is a blind start. Approximately one and a half hours after the track is laid, two tracklayers will cross over the track at two different places to test the dog's ability to stay with the original track. There will be at least two obstacles on the track such as a change of cover, fences, creeks, ditches, etc. The dog must have a TD before entering a TDX. There is no certification required for a TDX.

Variable Surface Tracking—VST

This test came into effect September 1995. The dog must have a TD earned at least six months prior to entering this test. The track is 600 to 800 yards long and shall have a minimum of three different surfaces. Vegetation shall be included along with two areas devoid of vegetation such as concrete, asphalt, gravel, sand, hard pan or mulch. The areas devoid of vegetation shall comprise at least one-third to one-half of the track. The track is aged three to five hours. There will be four to eight turns and four numbered articles including one leather, one plastic, one metal and one fabric dropped on the track. There is one starting flag. The handler will work at least 10 feet from the dog.

Action-packed agility competitions test a dog's coordination. Here, Moorelake Crosby's American Dream comes off the teeter totter.

AGILITY

Agility was first introduced by John Varley in England at the Crufts Dog Show, February 1978, but Peter Meanwell, competitor and judge, actually developed the idea. It was officially recognized in the early '80s. Agility is extremely popular in England and Canada and growing in popularity in the U.S. The AKC acknowledged agility in August 1994. Dogs must be at least 12 months of age to be entered. It is a fascinating sport that the dog, handler and spectators enjoy to the utmost. Agility is a spectator sport! The dog performs off lead. The handler either runs with his dog or positions himself on the course and directs his dog with verbal and hand signals over a timed course over or through a variety of obstacles including a time out or pause. One of the main drawbacks to agility is finding a place to train. The obstacles take up a lot of space and it is very time consuming to put up and take down courses.

A Golden Retriever clears a bar in agility. Agility is definitely a spectator sport!

The titles earned at AKC agility trials are Novice Agility Dog (NAD), Open Agility Dog (OAD), Agility Dog Excellent (ADX), and Master Agility Excellent (MAX). In order to acquire an agility title, a dog must earn a qualifying score in its respective class on three separate occasions under two different judges. The MAX will be awarded after earning ten qualifying scores in the Agility Excellent Class.

PERFORMANCE TESTS

During the last decade the American Kennel Club has promoted performance tests–those events that test the different breeds' natural abilities. This type of event encourages a handler to devote even more time to his dog and retain the natural instincts of his breed heritage. It is an important part of the wonderful world of dogs.

Hunting Titles

For retrievers, pointing breeds and spaniels. Titles offered are Junior Hunter (JH), Senior Hunter (SH), and Master Hunter (MH).

Flushing Spaniels Their primary purpose is to hunt, find, flush and return birds to hand as quickly as possible in a pleasing and obedient manner. The entrant must be at least six months of age and dogs with limited registration (ILP) are eligible. Game used are pigeons, pheasants, and quail.

Retrievers Limited registration (ILP) retrievers are not eligible to compete in Hunting Tests. The purpose of a Hunting Test for retrievers is to test the merits of and evaluate the abilities of retrievers in the field in order to determine their suitability and ability as hunting companions. They are

expected to retrieve any type of game bird, pheasants, ducks, pigeons, guinea hens and quail.

Pointing Breeds Are eligible at six months of age, and dogs with limited registration (ILP) are permitted. They must show a keen desire to hunt; be bold and independent; have a fast, yet attractive, manner of hunting; and demonstrate intelligence not only in seeking objectives but also in the ability to find game. They must establish point, and in the more advanced tests they need to be steady to wing and must remain in position until the bird is shot or they are released.

A Senior Hunter must retrieve. A Master Hunter must honor. The judges and the marshal are permitted to ride horseback during the test, but all handling must be done on foot.

General Information

Obedience, tracking and agility allow the purebred dog with an Indefinite Listing Privilege (ILP) number or a limited registration to be exhibited and earn titles. Application must be made to the AKC for an ILP number.

The American Kennel Club publishes a monthly *Events* magazine that is part of the *Gazette*, their official journal for the sport of purebred dogs. The *Events* section lists upcoming shows and the secretary or superintendent for them. The majority of the conformation shows in the U.S. are overseen by licensed superintendents. Generally the entry closing date is approximately two-and-a-half weeks before the actual show. Point shows are fairly expensive, while the match shows cost about one third of the point show entry fee. Match shows usually take entries the day of the show but some are pre-entry. The best way to find match show information is through your

Golden Retriever Ski Hi Montana Roper, CD, retrieves a duck in the Junior Hunter test.

local kennel club. Upon asking, the AKC can provide you with a list of superintendents, and you can write and ask to be put on their mailing lists.

Obedience trial and tracking test information is available through the AKC. Frequently these events are not superintended, but put on by the host club. Therefore you would make the entry with the event's secretary.

As you have read, there are numerous activities you can share with your dog. Regardless what you do, it does take teamwork. Your dog can only benefit from your attention and training. I hope this chapter has enlightened you and hope, if nothing else, you will attend a show here and there. Perhaps you will start with a puppy kindergarten class, and who knows where it may lead!

Retrievers are expected to retrieve in water as well as on land, and to bring back any type of game bird.

Hunting tests measure a retriever's skill in the field to determine if he is a suitable and competent hunting companion.

HEALTH CARE for the Golden Retriever

Veterinary medicine has become far more sophisticated than what was available to our ancestors. This can be attributed to the increase in household pets and consequently the demand for better care for them. Also human medicine has become far more complex. Today diagnostic testing in veterinary medicine parallels human diagnostics. Because of better technology we can expect our pets to live healthier lives thereby increasing their life spans.

THE FIRST CHECK UP

You will want to take your new puppy/dog in for its first check up within 48 to 72 hours after acquiring it. Many breeders strongly recommend this check up and so do the humane shelters. A puppy/dog can appear healthy but it may have a serious problem that is not apparent to the layman. Most pets have some type of a minor flaw that may never cause a real problem.

Unfortunately if he/she should have a serious problem, you will want to consider the consequences of keeping the pet and the attachments that will be formed, which may be broken prematurely. Keep in mind there are many healthy dogs looking for good homes.

This first check up is a good time to establish yourself with

Before you bring your puppy home, find a reputable veterinarian in your area. Be sure to obtain the puppy's health records from the breeder.

the veterinarian and learn the office policy regarding their hours and how they handle emergencies. Usually the breeder or another conscientious pet owner is a good reference for locating a capable veterinarian. You should be aware that not all veterinarians give the same quality of service. Please do not make your selection on the least expensive clinic, as they may be short changing your pet. There is the possibility that eventually it will cost you more due to improper diagnosis, treatment, etc. If you are selecting a new veterinarian, feel free to ask for a tour of the clinic.

Good veterinary care as a puppy will help your Golden grow into a strong and healthy adult.

Your Golden Retriever should receive an annual booster vaccination.

You should inquire about making an appointment for a tour since all clinics are working clinics, and therefore may not be available all day for sightseers. You may worry less if you see where your pet will be spending the day if he ever needs to be hospitalized.

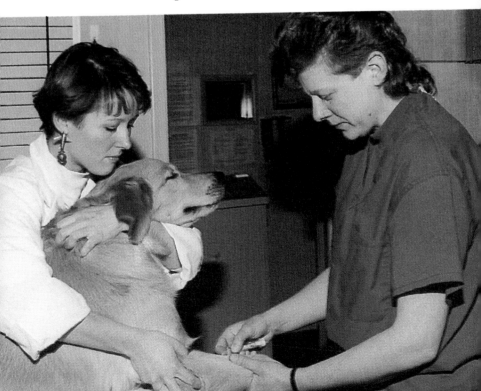

The Physical Exam

Your veterinarian will check your pet's overall condition, which includes listening to the heart; checking the respiration; feeling the abdomen, muscles and joints; checking the mouth, which includes the gum color and signs of gum disease along with plaque buildup; checking the ears for signs of an infection or ear mites; examining the eyes; and, last but not least, checking the condition of the skin and coat.

These five-week-old Golden Retriever puppies are at the proper age to begin receiving DHLPP and bordetella vaccinations.

He should ask you questions regarding your pet's eating and elimination habits and invite you to relay your questions. It is a good idea to prepare a list so as not to forget anything. He should discuss the proper diet and the quantity to be fed. If this should differ from your breeder's recommendation, then you should convey to him the breeder's choice and see if he approves. If he recommends changing the diet, then this should be done over a few days so as not to cause a gastrointestinal upset. It is customary to take in a fresh stool sample (just a small amount) for a test for intestinal parasites. It must be fresh, preferably within 12 hours, since the eggs hatch quickly and after hatching will not be observed under the microscope. If your pet isn't obliging then, usually the technician can take one in the clinic.

Immunizations

It is important that you take your puppy/dog's vaccination record with you on your first visit. In case of a puppy, presumably the breeder has seen to the vaccinations up to the time you acquired custody. Veterinarians differ in their vaccination protocol. It is not unusual for your puppy to have received vaccinations for distemper, hepatitis, leptospirosis, parvovirus and parainfluenza every

Plan a trip to the veterinarian soon after bringing your Golden puppy home. Regular physical exams will help to maintain your dog's health throughout his life.

two to three weeks from the age of five or six weeks. Usually this is a combined injection and is typically called the DHLPP. The DHLPP is given through at least 12 to 14 weeks of age, and it is customary to continue with another parvovirus vaccine at 16 to 18 weeks. You may wonder why so many immunizations are necessary. No one knows for sure when the puppy's maternal antibodies are gone, although it is customarily accepted that distemper antibodies are gone by 12 weeks. Usually parvovirus antibodies are gone by 16 to 18 weeks of age. However, it is possible for the maternal antibodies to be gone at a much earlier age or even a later age. Therefore immunizations are started at an early age. The vaccine will not give immunity as long as there are maternal antibodies.

The rabies vaccination is given at three or six months of age depending on your local laws. A vaccine for bordetella (kennel cough) is advisable and can be given anytime from the age of five weeks. The coronavirus is not commonly given unless there is a problem locally. The Lyme vaccine is necessary in endemic areas. Lyme disease has been reported in 47 states.

Distemper

This is virtually an incurable disease. If the dog recovers, he is subject to severe nervous disorders. The virus attacks every tissue in the body and resembles a bad cold with a fever. It can cause a runny nose and eyes and cause gastrointestinal disorders, including a poor appetite, vomiting and diarrhea. The virus is carried by raccoons, foxes, wolves, mink and other dogs. Unvaccinated youngsters and senior citizens are very susceptible. This is still a common disease.

Hepatitis

This is a virus that is most serious in very young dogs. It is spread by contact with an infected animal or its stool or urine. The virus affects the liver and kidneys and is characterized by high fever, depression and lack of appetite. Recovered animals may be afflicted with chronic illnesses.

Leptospirosis

This is a bacterial disease transmitted by contact with the urine of an infected dog, rat or other wildlife. It produces severe symptoms of fever, depression, jaundice and internal bleeding and was fatal before the vaccine was developed. Recovered dogs can be carriers, and the disease can be transmitted from dogs to humans.

Parvovirus

This was first noted in the late 1970s and is still a fatal disease. However, with proper vaccinations, early diagnosis and prompt treatment, it is a manageable disease. It attacks the bone marrow and intestinal tract. The symptoms include depression, loss of appetite, vomiting, diarrhea and collapse. Immediate medical attention is of the essence.

Maternal antibodies protect puppies from disease in the first weeks of their lives. Vaccinations are necessary because the antibodies are only temporarily effective.

Rabies

This is shed in the saliva and is carried by raccoons, skunks, foxes, other dogs and cats. It attacks nerve tissue, resulting in paralysis and death. Rabies can be transmitted to people and is virtually always fatal. This disease is reappearing in the suburbs.

Bordetella (Kennel Cough)

The symptoms are coughing, sneezing, hacking and retching accompanied by nasal discharge usually lasting from a few days to several weeks. There are several disease-producing organisms responsible for this disease. The present vaccines are helpful but do not protect for all the strains. It usually is not life threatening but in some instances it can progress to a serious bronchopneumonia. The disease is highly contagious. The vaccination should be given routinely for dogs that come in contact with other dogs, such as through boarding, training class or visits to the groomer.

Coronavirus

This is usually self limiting and not life threatening. It was first noted in the late '70s about a year before parvovirus. The virus produces a yellow/brown stool and there may be depression, vomiting and diarrhea.

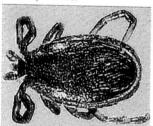

Ticks have forever been a common parasite of both man and dog. Courtesy of Virbac Laboratories, Inc., Fort Worth, Texas.

Lyme Disease

This was first diagnosed in the United States in 1976 in Lyme, CT in people who lived in close proximity to the deer tick. Symptoms may include acute lameness, fever, swelling of joints and loss of appetite. Your veterinarian can advise you if you live in an endemic area.

After your puppy has completed his puppy vaccinations, you will continue to booster the DHLPP once a year. It is customary to booster the rabies one year after the first vaccine and then, depending on where you live, it should be boostered every year or every three years. This depends on your local laws. The Lyme and corona vaccines are boostered annually and it is recommended that the bordetella be boostered every six to eight months.

ANNUAL VISIT

I would like to impress the importance of the annual check up, which would include the booster vaccinations, check for

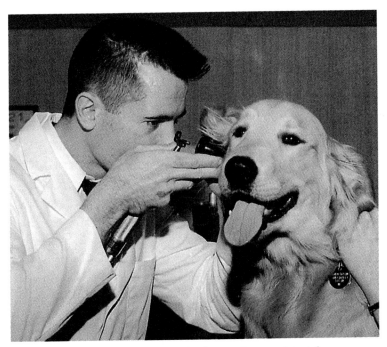

Your dog's annual visit to the veterinarian will include a physical exam and a thorough inspection of the ears. intestinal parasites and test for heartworm. Today in our very busy world it is rush, rush and see "how much you can get for how little." Unbelievably, some non-veterinary businesses have entered into the vaccination business. More harm than good can come to your dog through improper vaccinations, possibly from inferior vaccines and/or the wrong schedule. More than likely you truly care about your companion dog and over the years you have devoted much time and expense to his well being. Perhaps you are unaware that a vaccination is not just a vaccination. There is more involved. Please, please follow through with regular physical examinations. It is so important for your veterinarian to know your dog and this is especially true during middle age through the geriatric years. More than likely your older dog will require more than one physical a year. The annual physical is good preventive medicine. Through early diagnosis and subsequent treatment your dog can maintain a longer and better quality of life.

Think of your dog's annual check-up as preventive medicine. Early detection and early treatment of any problems will result in better health for your dog.

INTESTINAL PARASITES

Hookworms

These are almost microscopic intestinal worms that can cause anemia and therefore serious problems, including death, in young puppies. Hookworms can be transmitted to humans through penetration of the skin. Puppies may be born with them.

Roundworms

These are spaghetti-like worms that can cause a potbellied appearance and dull coat along with more severe symptoms, such as vomiting, diarrhea and coughing. Puppies acquire these while in the mother's uterus and through lactation. Both hookworms and roundworms may be acquired through ingestion.

Whipworms

These have a three-month life cycle and are not acquired through the dam. They cause intermittent diarrhea usually with mucus. Whipworms are possibly the most difficult worm to eradicate. Their eggs are very resistant to most environmental factors and can last for years until the proper conditions enable them to mature. Whipworms are seldom seen in the stool.

Intestinal parasites are more prevalent in some areas than others. Climate, soil and contamination are big factors contributing to the incidence of intestinal parasites. Eggs are passed in the stool, lay on the ground and then become infective in a certain number of days. Each of the above worms has a different life cycle. Your best chance of becoming and remaining worm-free is to always pooper-scoop your yard. A fenced-in yard keeps stray dogs out, which is certainly helpful.

Whipworms are hard to find unless one strains the feces, and this is best left to a veterinarian. Pictured here are adult whipworms.

I would recommend having a fecal examination on your dog twice a year or more often if there is a problem. If your dog has a positive fecal sample, then he will be given the appropriate medication and you will be asked to bring back another stool sample in a certain period of time (depending on the type of worm) and then be rewormed. This process goes on until he has at least two negative samples. The different types of worms require different medications. You will be wasting your money and doing your dog an injustice by buying over-the-counter medication without first consulting your veterinarian.

OTHER INTERNAL PARASITES

Coccidiosis and Giardiasis

These protozoal infections usually affect puppies, especially in places where large numbers of puppies are brought together. Older dogs may harbor these infections but do not show signs unless they are stressed. Symptoms include diarrhea, weight loss and lack of appetite. These infections are not always apparent in the fecal examination.

Tapeworms

Seldom apparent on fecal floatation, they are diagnosed frequently as rice-like segments around the dog's anus and the base of the tail. Tapeworms are long, flat and ribbon like, sometimes several feet in length, and made up of many segments about five-eighths of an inch long. The two most common types of tapeworms found in the dog are:

(1) First the larval form of the flea tapeworm parasite must mature in an intermediate host, the flea, before it can become infective. Your dog acquires this by ingesting the flea through licking and chewing.

(2) Rabbits, rodents and certain large game animals serve as intermediate hosts for other species of tapeworms. If your dog should eat one of these infected hosts, then he can acquire tapeworms.

HEARTWORM DISEASE

This is a worm that resides in the heart and adjacent blood vessels of the lung that produces microfilaria, which circulate in the bloodstream. It is possible for a dog to be infected with

The more time puppies spend outside, the more chance they have of picking up parasites. Make sure to check often for both internal and external parasites.

any number of worms from one to a hundred that can be 6 to 14 inches long. It is a life-threatening disease, expensive to treat and easily prevented. Depending on where you live, your veterinarian may recommend a preventive year-round and either an annual or semiannual blood test. The most common preventive is given once a month.

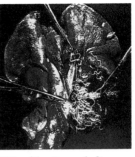

Dirofilaria—adult worms in heart of a dog. It is possible for a dog to be infected with any number of worms from one to a hundred. Courtesy of Merck AgVet.

EXTERNAL PARASITES

Fleas

These pests are not only the dog's worst enemy but also enemy to the owner's pocketbook. Preventing is less expensive than treating, but regardless I think we'd prefer to spend our money elsewhere. I would guess that the majority of our dogs

Diagram of the cat flea. Courtesy of Fleabusters, Rx for Fleas, Inc., Fort Lauderdale, Florida.

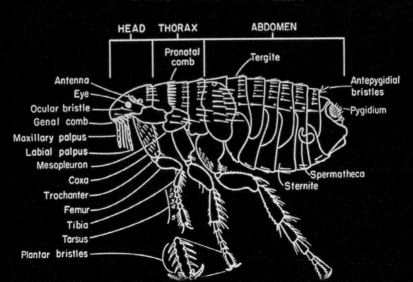

DIAGRAM OF FLEA

HEAD THORAX ABDOMEN

Pronotal comb
Tergite

Antenna
Eye
Ocular bristle
Genal comb
Maxillary palpus
Labial palpus
Mesopleuron
Coxa
Trochanter
Femur
Tibia
Tarsus
Plantar bristles

Antepygidial bristles
Pygidium
Spermatheca
Sternite

are allergic to the bite of a flea, and in many cases it only takes one flea bite. The protein in the flea's saliva is the culprit. Allergic dogs have a reaction, which usually results in a "hot spot." More than likely such a reaction will involve a trip to the veterinarian for treatment. Yes, prevention is less expensive. Fortunately today there are several good products available.

Dogs are more susceptible to fleas in warmer weather—keep this in mind during the spring and summer months.

If there is a flea infestation, no one product is going to correct the problem. Not only will the dog require treatment so will the environment. In general flea collars are not very effective although there is now available an "egg" collar that will kill the eggs on the dog. Dips are the most economical but they are messy. There are some effective shampoos and treatments available through pet shops and veterinarians. An oral tablet arrived on the American market in 1995 and was popular in Europe the previous year. It sterilizes the female flea but will not kill adult fleas. Therefore the tablet, which is given monthly, will decrease the flea population but is not a "cure-all." Those dogs that suffer from flea-bite allergy will still be subjected to the bite of the flea. Another popular parasiticide is permethrin, which is applied to the back of the dog in one or two places depending on the dog's weight. This product works as a repellent causing the flea to get "hot feet" and jump off. Do not confuse this product with some of the organophosphates that are also applied to the dog's back.

Some products are not usable on young puppies. Treating fleas should be done under your veterinarian's guidance. Frequently it is necessary to combine products and the layman does not have the knowledge regarding possible toxicities. It is

hard to believe but there are a few dogs that do have a natural resistance to fleas. Nevertheless it would be wise to treat all pets at the

The cat flea is the most common flea of dogs. It starts feeding soon after it makes contact with the dog.

same time. Don't forget your cats. Cats just love to prowl the neighborhood and consequently return with unwanted guests.

Adult fleas live on the dog but their eggs drop off the dog into the environment. There they go through four larval stages before reaching adulthood, and thereby are able to jump back on the poor unsuspecting dog. The cycle resumes and takes between 21 to 28 days under ideal conditions. There are environmental products available that will kill both the adult fleas and the larvae.

Ticks

Ticks carry Rocky Mountain Spotted Fever, Lyme disease and can cause tick paralysis. They should be removed with tweezers, trying to pull out the head. The jaws carry disease. There is a tick preventive collar that does an excellent job. The ticks automatically back out on those dogs wearing collars.

Sarcoptic Mange

This is a mite that is difficult to find on skin scrapings. The pinnal reflex is a good indicator of this disease. Rub the ends of the pinna (ear) together and the dog will start scratching with his foot. Sarcoptes are highly contagious to other dogs and to humans although they do not live long on humans. They cause intense itching.

Demodectic Mange

This is a mite that is passed from the dam to her puppies. It affects youngsters age three to ten months. Diagnosis is confirmed by skin scraping. Small areas of alopecia around the eyes, lips and/or forelegs become visible. There is little itching unless there is a secondary bacterial infection. Some breeds are afflicted more than others.

Cheyletiella

This causes intense itching and is diagnosed by skin scraping. It lives in the outer layers of the skin of dogs, cats, rabbits and humans. Yellow-gray scales may be found on the back and the rump, top of the head and the nose.

To Breed or Not To Breed

More than likely your breeder has requested that you have your puppy neutered or spayed. Your breeder's request is based on what is healthiest for your dog and what is most beneficial for your breed. Experienced and conscientious breeders devote many years into developing a bloodline. In order to do this, he makes every effort to plan each breeding in regard to conformation, temperament and health. This type of breeder does his best to perform the necessary testing (i.e., OFA, CERF, testing for inherited blood disorders, thyroid, etc.). Testing is expensive and sometimes very disheartening when a favorite dog doesn't pass his health tests. The health history pertains not only to the breeding stock but to the immediate ancestors. Reputable breeders do not want their offspring to

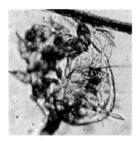

A sarcoptic mite is the culprit of "scabies." This is probably the itchiest condition that affects dogs.

be bred indiscriminately. Therefore you may be asked to neuter or spay your puppy. Of course there is always the exception, and your breeder may agree to let you breed your dog under his direct supervision. This is an important concept. More and more effort is being made to breed healthier dogs.

Spay/Neuter

There are numerous benefits of performing this surgery at six months of age. Unspayed females are subject to mammary and ovarian cancer. In order to prevent mammary cancer she must be spayed prior to her first heat cycle. Later in life, an unspayed female may develop a pyometra (an infected uterus), which is definitely life threatening.

Spaying is performed under a general anesthetic and is easy on the young dog. As you might expect it is a little harder on the older dog, but that is no reason to deny her the surgery. The surgery removes the ovaries and uterus. It is important to remove all the ovarian tissue. If some is left behind, she could remain attractive to males. In order to view the ovaries, a reasonably long incision is necessary. An ovariohysterectomy is considered major surgery.

Neutering the male at a young age will inhibit some characteristic male behavior that owners frown upon. I have found my boys will not hike their legs and mark territory if they are neutered at six months of age. Also neutering at a young age has hormonal benefits, lessening the chance of hormonal aggressiveness.

Surgery involves removing the testicles but leaving the scrotum. If there should be a retained testicle, then he definitely needs to be neutered before the age of two or three years. Retained testicles can develop into cancer. Unneutered males are at risk for testicular cancer, perineal fistulas, perianal tumors and fistulas and prostatic disease.

Intact males and females are prone to housebreaking accidents. Females urinate frequently before, during and after heat cycles, and males tend to mark territory if there is a female in heat. Males may show the same behavior if there is a visiting dog or guests.

Alhtough these five-week-old puppies are cute, once they awaken they will need a lot of care and attention.

Surgery involves a sterile operating procedure equivalent to human surgery.

Having your dog spayed or neutered can lessen the risk of certain health problems, giving you a healthy, long-lived family companion.

The incision site is shaved, surgically scrubbed and draped. The veterinarian wears a sterile surgical gown, cap, mask and gloves. Anesthesia should be monitored by a registered technician. It is customary for the veterinarian to recommend a pre-anesthetic blood screening, looking for metabolic problems and a ECG rhythm strip to check for normal heart function. Today anesthetics are equal to human anesthetics, which enables your dog to walk out of the clinic the same day as surgery.

Some folks worry about their dog gaining weight after being neutered or spayed. This is usually not the case. It is true that some dogs may be less active so they could develop a problem, but my own dogs are just as active as they were before surgery. I have a hard time keeping weight on them. However, if your dog should begin to gain, then you need to decrease his food and see to it that he gets a little more exercise.

DENTAL CARE for Your Dog's Life

So you've got a new puppy! You also have a new set of puppy teeth in your household. Anyone who has ever raised a puppy is abundantly aware of these new teeth. Your puppy will chew anything it can reach, chase your shoelaces, and play "tear the rag" with any piece of clothing it can find. When puppies are newly born, they have no teeth. At about four weeks of age, puppies of most breeds begin to develop their deciduous or baby teeth. They begin eating semi-solid food, fighting and biting with their litter mates, and learning discipline from their mother. As their new teeth come in, they inflict more pain on their mother's breasts, so her feeding sessions become less frequent and shorter. By six or eight weeks, the mother will start growling to warn her pups when they are fighting too roughly or hurting her as they nurse too much with their new teeth.

Gumabone® products, due to their softer consistency, are excellent chew toys for puppies and less powerful chewers.

Puppies need to chew. It is a necessary part of their physical and mental development. They develop muscles and necessary life skills as they drag objects around, fight over possession, and vocalize alerts and warnings. Puppies chew on things to explore their world. They are using their sense of taste to determine what is food and what is not. How else can they tell an electrical cord from a lizard? At about four months of age, most puppies begin shedding their baby teeth. Often these teeth need some help to come out and make way for the permanent teeth. The incisors (front teeth) will be replaced first. Then, the adult canine or fang teeth erupt. When the baby tooth is not shed before the permanent tooth comes in, veterinarians call it a retained

This Golden is chewing on a Gumabone® Tug Toy®. Also pictured is the Hercules® bone, which is covered with raised plaque-fighting dental tips.

deciduous tooth. This condition will often cause gum infections by trapping hair and debris between the permanent tooth and the retained baby tooth. Nylafloss® is an excellent device for puppies to use. They can toss it, drag it, and chew on the many surfaces it presents. The baby teeth can catch in the nylon material, aiding in their removal. Puppies that have adequate chew toys will have less destructive behavior, develop more physically, and have less chance of retained deciduous teeth.

During the first year, your dog should be seen by your veterinarian at regular intervals. Your veterinarian will let you know when to bring in your puppy for vaccinations and parasite examinations. At each visit, your veterinarian should inspect the lips, teeth, and mouth as part of a complete physical examination. You should take some part in the maintenance of your dog's oral health. You should examine your dog's mouth weekly throughout his first year to make sure there are no sores, foreign objects, tooth problems, etc. If your dog drools excessively, shakes its head, or has bad breath, consult your veterinarian. By the time your dog is six months old, the permanent teeth are all in and plaque can start to accumulate on the tooth surfaces. This is when your dog needs to develop good dental-care habits to prevent calculus build-up on its teeth. Brushing is best. That is a fact that cannot be denied. However, some dogs do not like their teeth brushed regularly, or you may not be able to accomplish the task. In that case, you should consider a product that will help prevent plaque and calculus build-up.

The Plaque Attackers® and Galileo Bone® are other excellent choices for the first three years of a dog's life. Their shapes make them interesting for the dog. As the dog chews on them, the solid polyurethane massages the gums which improves the blood circulation to the periodontal tissues. Projections on the chew devices increase the surface and are in contact with the tooth for more efficient cleaning. The unique shape and consistency prevent your dog from exerting excessive force on his own teeth or from breaking off pieces of the bone. If your dog is an aggressive chewer or weighs more than 55 pounds (25 kg), you should consider giving him a Nylabone®, the most durable chew product on the market.

The Gumabones®, made by the Nylabone Company, is constructed of strong polyurethane, which is softer than nylon. Less powerful chewers prefer the Gumabones® to the Nylabones®. A super option for your dog is the Hercules Bone®, a uniquely shaped bone named after the great Olympian for its exceptional strength. Like all Nylabone products, they are specially scented to make them attractive to your dog. Ask your veterinarian about these bones and he will validate the good doctor's prescription: Nylabones® not only

A Golden Retriever munches on a crunchy Chooz® treat. Chooz® are edible treats which help to clean the dog's teeth as he chews.

Puppies love to chew—wouldn't you rather he chew on a Gumabone® than on your shoelaces?

give your dog a good chewing workout but also help to save your dog's teeth (and even his life, as it protects him from possible fatal periodontal diseases).

By the time dogs are four years old, 75% of them have periodontal disease. It is the most common infection in dogs. Yearly examinations by your veterinarian are essential to maintaining your dog's good health. If your veterinarian detects periodontal disease, he or she may recommend a prophylactic cleaning. To do a thorough cleaning, it will be necessary to put your dog under anesthesia. With modern gas anesthetics and monitoring equipment, the procedure is pretty safe. Your veterinarian will scale the teeth with an ultrasound scaler or hand instrument. This removes the calculus from the teeth. If there are calculus deposits below the gum line, the veterinarian will plane the roots to make them smooth. After all of the calculus has been removed, the teeth are polished with pumice in a polishing cup. If any medical or surgical treatment is needed, it is done at this time. The final step would be fluoride treatment and your follow-up treatment at home. If the periodontal disease is advanced, the veterinarian may prescribe a medicated mouth rinse or antibiotics for use at home. Make sure your dog has safe, clean and attractive chew toys and treats. Chooz® treats are another way of using a consumable treat to help keep your dog's teeth clean.

Rawhide is the most popular of all materials for a dog to chew. This has never been good news to dog owners, because rawhide is inherently very dangerous for dogs. Thousands of dogs have died from rawhide, having swallowed the hide after it has become soft and mushy, only to cause stomach and intestinal blockage. A new rawhide product on the market has finally solved the problem of rawhide: molded Roar-Hide™ from Nylabone. These are composed of processed, cut up, and melted American rawhide injected into your dog's favorite shape: a dog bone. These dog-safe devices smell and taste like rawhide but don't break up. The ridges on the bones help to fight tartar build-up on the teeth and they last ten times longer than the usual rawhide chews.

Larger dogs and more aggressive chewers will benefit from the Nylabone®, the most durable chew product on the market.

The Gumabone® Frisbee® has a dog bone molded on top to make it easier for the dog to pick up when it lands on a flat surface.*

The trademark Frisbee is used under license from Mattel, Inc., CA, USA.

As your dog ages, professional examination and cleaning should become more frequent. The mouth should be inspected at least once a year. Your veterinarian may recommend visits every six months. In the geriatric patient, organs such as the heart, liver, and kidneys do not function as well as when they were young. Your veterinarian will probably want to test these organs' functions prior to using general anesthesia for dental cleaning. If your dog is a good chewer and you work closely with your veterinarian, your dog can keep all of its teeth all of its life. However, as your dog ages, his sense of smell, sight, and taste will diminish. He may not have the desire to chase, trap or chew his toys. He will also not have the energy to chew for long periods, as arthritis and periodontal disease make chewing painful. This will leave you with more responsibility for keeping his teeth clean and healthy. The dog that would not let you brush his teeth at one year of age, may let you brush his teeth now that he is ten years old.

If you train your dog with good chewing habits as a puppy, he will have healthier teeth throughout his life.

IDENTIFICATION and Finding the Lost Dog

There are several ways of identifying your dog. The old standby is a collar with dog license, rabies, and ID tags. Unfortunately collars have a way of being separated from the dog and tags fall off. I am not suggesting you shouldn't use a collar and tags. If they stay intact and on the dog, they are the quickest way of identification.

For several years owners have been tattooing their dogs. Some tattoos use a number with a registry. Here lies the problem because there are several registries to check. If you wish to tattoo, use your social security number. The humane shelters have the means to trace it. It is usually done on the inside of the rear thigh. The area is first shaved and numbed. There is no pain, although a few dogs do not like the buzzing sound. Occasionally tattooing is not legible and needs to be redone.

The newest method of identification is microchipping. The microchip is a computer chip that is no larger than a grain of rice. The veterinarian implants it by injection between the shoulder blades. The dog feels no discomfort. If your dog is lost and picked up by the humane society, they can trace you by scanning the microchip, which has its own code. Microchip scanners are friendly to other brands of microchips and their registries. The microchip comes with a dog tag saying the dog is microchipped. It is the safest way of identifying your dog.

FINDING THE LOST DOG

I am sure you will agree with me that there would be little worse than losing your dog. Responsible pet owners rarely lose their dogs. They do not let their dogs run free because they don't want harm to come to them. Not only that but in most, if not all, states there is a leash law.

Beware of fenced-in yards. They can be a hazard. Dogs find ways to escape either over or under the fence. Another fast exit is through the gate that perhaps the neighbor's child left unlocked.

Below is a list that hopefully will be of help to you if you need it. Remember don't give up, keep looking. Your dog is worth your efforts.

1. Contact your neighbors and put flyers with a photo on it in their mailboxes. Information you should include would be the dog's name, breed, sex, color, age, source of identification, when your dog was last seen and where, and your name and phone numbers. It may be helpful to say the dog needs medical care. Offer a *reward*.

2. Check all local shelters daily. It is also possible for your dog to be picked up away from home and end up in an out-of-the-way shelter. Check these too. Go in person. It is not good enough to call. Most shelters are limited on the time they can hold dogs then they are put up for adoption or euthanized. There is the possibility that your dog will not make it to the shelter for several days. Your dog could have been wandering or someone may have tried to keep him.

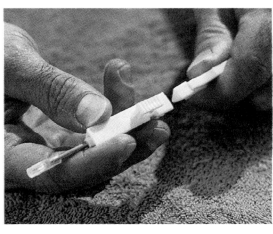

A microchip is painlessly implanted between the dog's shoulder blades. When scanned, the microchip will trace the dog to his owner.

3. Notify all local veterinarians. Call and send flyers.

4. Call your breeder. Frequently breeders are contacted when one of their breed is found.

5. Contact the rescue group for your breed.

6. Contact local schools—children may have seen your dog.

7. Post flyers at the schools, groceries, gas stations, convenience stores, veterinary clinics, groomers and any other place that will allow them.

8. Advertise in the newspaper.

9. Advertise on the radio.

TRAVELING with Your Dog

The earlier you start traveling with your new puppy or dog, the better. He needs to become accustomed to traveling. However, some dogs are nervous riders and become carsick easily. It is helpful if he starts with an empty stomach. Do not despair, as it will go better if you continue taking him with you on short fun rides. How would you feel if every time you rode in the car you stopped at the doctor's for an injection? You would soon dread that nasty car. Older dogs that tend to get carsick may have more of a problem adjusting to traveling. Those dogs that are having a serious problem may benefit from some medication prescribed by the veterinarian.

A reputable boarding kennel will require that dogs receive the vaccination for kennel cough no less than two weeks before their scheduled stay.

Do give your dog a chance to relieve himself before getting into the car. It is a good idea to be prepared for a clean up with a leash, paper towels, bag and terry cloth towel.

The safest place for your dog is in a fiberglass crate, although close confinement can promote carsickness in some dogs. If your dog is nervous you can try letting him ride on the seat next to you or in someone's lap.

An alternative to the crate would be to use a car harness made for dogs and/or a safety strap attached to the harness or collar. Whatever you do, do not let your dog ride in the back of a pickup truck unless he is securely tied on a very short lead. I've seen trucks stop quickly and, even though the dog was tied, it fell out and was dragged.

I do occasionally let my dogs ride loose with me because I

If you are taking a long trip with your dog, bring some water from home with you. Your dog will get thirsty, and it is best to give him water that he is used to.

really enjoy their companionship, but in all honesty they are safer in their crates. I have a friend whose van rolled in an accident but his dogs, in their fiberglass crates, were not injured nor did they escape. Another advantage of the crate is that it is a safe place to leave him if you need to run into the store. Otherwise you wouldn't be able to leave the windows down. Keep in mind that while many dogs are overly protective in their crates, this may not be enough to deter dognappers. In some states it is against the law to leave a dog in the car unattended.

Never leave a dog loose in the car wearing a collar and leash. I have known more than one dog that has killed himself by hanging. Do not let him put his head out an open window. Foreign debris can be blown into his eyes. When leaving your dog unattended in a car, consider the temperature. It can take less than five minutes to reach temperatures over 100 degrees Fahrenheit.

TRIPS

Perhaps you are taking a trip. Give consideration to what is best for your dog—traveling with you or boarding. When traveling by car, van or motor home, you need to think ahead about locking your vehicle. In all probability you have many valuables in the car and do not wish to leave it unlocked. Perhaps most valuable and not replaceable is your dog. Give thought to securing your vehicle and providing adequate ventilation for him. Another consideration for you when traveling with your dog is medical problems that may arise and little inconveniences, such as exposure to external parasites. Some areas of the country are quite flea infested. You may want to carry flea spray with you. This is even a good idea when staying in motels. Quite possibly you are not the only occupant of the room.

Unbelievably many motels and even hotels do allow canine guests, even some very first-class ones. Gaines Pet Foods Corporation publishes *Touring With Towser*, a directory of domestic hotels and motels that accommodate guests with

dogs. Their address is Gaines TWT, PO Box 5700, Kankakee, IL, 60902. I would recommend you call ahead to any motel that you may be considering and see if they accept pets. Sometimes it is necessary to pay a deposit against room damage. Of course you are more likely to gain accommodations for a small dog than a large dog. Also the management feels reassured when you mention that your dog will be crated. Since my dogs tend to bark when I leave the room, I leave the TV on nearly full blast to deaden

Four Paws Pet Safety Sitter is designed to protect dogs from injury by securing them in place and preventing them from disturbing drivers and passengers.

Crates are a safe way for your dog to travel. The fiberglass crates are safest but the metal crates allow more air.

the noises outside that tend to encourage my dogs to bark. If you do travel with your dog, take along plenty of baggies so that you can clean up after him. When we all do our share in cleaning up, we make it possible for motels to continue accepting our pets. As a matter of fact, you should practice cleaning up everywhere you take your dog.

Depending on where your are traveling, you may need an up-to-date health certificate issued by your veterinarian. It is good policy to take along your dog's medical information, which would include the name, address and phone number of your veterinarian, vaccination record, rabies certificate, and any medication he is taking.

AIR TRAVEL

When traveling by air, you need to contact the airlines to check their policy. Usually you have to make arrangements up to a couple of weeks in advance for traveling with your dog. The airlines require your dog to travel in an airline approved fiberglass crate. Usually these can be purchased through the airlines but they are also readily available in most pet-supply stores. If your dog is not accustomed to a crate, then it is a good idea to get him acclimated to it before your trip. The day of the actual trip you should withhold water about one hour ahead of departure and no food for about 12 hours. The airlines generally have temperature restrictions, which do not allow pets to travel if it is either too cold or too hot. Frequently these restrictions are based on the temperatures at the departure and arrival airports. It's best to inquire about a health certificate. These usually need to be issued within ten days of departure. You should arrange for non-stop, direct flights and if a commuter plane should be involved, check to see if it will carry dogs. Some don't. The Humane Society of the United States has put together a tip sheet for airline traveling. You can receive a copy by sending a self-addressed stamped envelope to:

The Humane Society of the United States
Tip Sheet
2100 L Street NW
Washington, DC 20037.

Regulations differ for traveling outside of the country and are sometimes changed without notice. Well in advance you need to write or call the appropriate consulate or agricultural department for instructions. Some countries have lengthy quarantines (six months), and countries differ in their rabies vaccination requirements. For instance, it may have to be given at least 30 days ahead of your departure.

Do make sure your dog is wearing proper identification. You never know when you might be in an accident and separated from your dog. Or your dog could be frightened and somehow manage to escape and run away. When I travel, my dogs wear collars with engraved nameplates with my name, phone number and city.

Another suggestion would be to carry in-case-of-emergency instructions. These would include the address and phone number of a relative or friend, your veterinarian's name, address and phone number, and your dog's medical information.

BOARDING KENNELS

Perhaps you have decided that you need to board your dog. Your veterinarian can recommend a good boarding facility or possibly a pet sitter that will come to your house. It is customary for the boarding kennel to ask for proof of vaccination for the DHLPP, rabies and bordetella vaccine. The bordetella should have been given within six months of boarding. This is for your protection. If they do not ask for this proof I would not board at their kennel. Ask about flea control. Those dogs that suffer flea-bite allergy can get in trouble at a boarding kennel. Unfortunately boarding kennels are limited on how much they are able to do.

For more information on pet sitting, contact NAPPS:
National Association of Professional Pet Sitters
1200 G Street, NW
Suite 760
Washington, DC 20005.

Our clinic has technicians that pet sit and technicians that board clinic patients in their homes. This may be an alternative for you. Ask your veterinarian if they have an employee that can help you. There is a definite advantage of having a technician care for your dog, especially if your dog is on medication or is a senior citizen.

You can write for a copy of *Traveling With Your Pet* from ASPCA, Education Department, 441 E. 92nd Street, New York, NY 10128.

The more accustomed he is to traveling, the happier your dog will be in the car. These Golden Retrievers are ready to go!

THE 8th DAY GOD CREATED
DEN RETRIEVERS

IT'S HARD TO BE HUMBLE
WHEN YOU OWN A
GOLDEN RETRIEVER

BEHAVIOR and Canine Communication

Studies of the human/animal bond point out the importance of the unique relationships that exist between people and their pets. Those of us who share our lives with pets understand the special part they play through companionship, service and protection.

Senior citizens show more concern for their own eating habits when they have the responsibility of feeding a dog. Seeing that their dog is routinely exercised encourages the owner to think of schedules that otherwise may seem unimportant to the senior citizen. The older owner may be arthritic and feeling poorly but with responsibility for his dog he has a reason to get up and get moving. It is a big plus if his dog is an attention seeker who will demand such from his owner.

Over the last couple of decades, it has been shown that pets relieve the stress of those who lead busy lives. Owning a pet has been known to lessen the occurrence of heart attack and stroke.

Many single folks thrive on the companionship of a dog. Lifestyles are very different from a long time ago, and today more individuals seek the single life. However, they receive fulfillment from owning a dog.

Most likely the majority of our dogs live in family environments. The companionship they provide is well worth the effort involved. In my opinion, every child should have the opportunity to have a family dog. Dogs teach responsibility through understanding their care, feelings and even respecting their life cycles. Frequently those children who have not been exposed to dogs grow up afraid of dogs, which isn't good. Dogs sense timidity and some will take advantage of the situation.

Today more dogs are serving as service dogs. Since the origination of the Seeing Eye dogs years ago, we now have trained hearing dogs. Also dogs are trained to provide service for the handicapped and are able to perform many different tasks for their owners. Search and Rescue dogs, with their handlers, are sent throughout the world to assist in recovery of disaster victims. They are life savers.

Therapy dogs are very popular with nursing homes, and some hospitals even allow them to visit. The inhabitants truly look forward to their visits. I have taken a couple of my dogs visiting and left in tears when I saw the response of the patients. They wanted and were allowed to have my dogs in their beds to hold and love.

Nationally there is a Pet Awareness Week to educate students and others about the value and basic care of our pets. Many countries take an even greater interest in their pets than Americans do. In those countries the pets are allowed to accompany their owners into restaurants and shops, etc. In the U.S. this freedom is only available to our service dogs. Even so we think very highly of the human/animal bond.

Caring for a dog can teach a child responsibility and provide her with a faithful friend. Children should not grow up being afraid of dogs.

CANINE BEHAVIOR

Canine behavior problems are the number-one reason for pet owners to dispose of their dogs, either through new homes, humane shelters or euthanasia. Unfortunately there are

too many owners who are unwilling to devote the necessary time to properly train their dogs. On the other hand, there are those who not only are concerned about inherited health problems but are also aware of the dog's mental stability.

You may realize that a breed and his group relatives (i.e., sporting, hounds, etc.) show tendencies to behavioral characteristics. An experienced breeder can acquaint you with his breed's personality. Unfortunately many breeds are labeled with poor temperaments when actually the breed as a whole is not affected but only a small percentage of individuals within the breed.

If the breed in question is very popular, then of course there may be a higher number of unstable dogs. Do not label a breed good or bad. I know of absolutely awful-tempered dogs within one of our most popular, lovable breeds.

Inheritance and environment contribute to the dog's behavior. Some naïve people suggest inbreeding as the cause of bad temperaments. Inbreeding only results in poor behavior if the ancestors carry the trait. If there are excellent temperaments behind the dogs, then inbreeding will promote good temperaments in the offspring. Did you ever consider that inbreeding is what sets the characteristics of a breed? A purebred dog is the end result of inbreeding. This does not spare the mixed-breed dog from the same problems. Mixed-breed dogs frequently are the offspring of purebred dogs.

When planning a breeding, I like to observe the potential stud and his offspring in the show ring. If I see unruly behavior, I try to look into it further. I want to know if it is genetic or environmental, due to the lack of training and socialization. A good breeder will avoid breeding mentally unsound dogs.

Not too many decades ago most of our dogs led a different lifestyle than what is prevalent today. Usually mom stayed home so the dog had human companionship and

Start focusing on behavior with your puppy right away—teach him what behavior is unacceptable and what makes you happy.

If your dog is crated or left in the house all day, make sure to give him time in the evening to exercise and release his energy. someone to discipline it if needed. Not much was expected from the dog. Today's mom works and everyone's life is at a much faster pace.

The dog may have to adjust to being a "weekend" dog. The family is gone all day during the week, and the dog is left to his own devices for entertainment. Some dogs sleep all day waiting for their family to come home and others become wigwam wreckers if given the opportunity. Crates do ensure the safety of the dog and the house. However, he could become a physically and emotionally cripple if he doesn't get enough exercise and attention. We still appreciate and want the companionship of our dogs although we expect more from them. In many cases we tend to forget dogs are just that—*dogs* not human beings.

I own several dogs who are left crated during the day but I do try to make time for them in the evenings and on the weekends. Also we try to do something together before I leave for work. Maybe it helps them to have the companionship of other dogs. They accept their crates as their personal "houses" and seem to be content with their routine and thrive on trying their best to please me.

Socializing and Training

Many prospective puppy buyers lack experience regarding the proper socialization and training needed to develop the type of pet we all desire. In the first 18 months, training does take some work. Trust me, it is easier to start proper training before there is a problem that needs to be corrected.

The initial work begins with the breeder. The breeder should start socializing the puppy at five to six weeks of age and cannot let up. Human socializing is critical up through 12 weeks of age and likewise important during the following months. The litter should be left together during the first few weeks but it is necessary to separate them by ten weeks of age. Leaving them together after that time will increase competition for litter dominance. If puppies are not socialized with people by 12 weeks of age, they will be timid in later life.

The eight- to ten-week age period is a fearful time for puppies. They need to be handled very gently around children and adults. There should be no harsh discipline during this time. Starting at 14 weeks of age, the puppy begins the juvenile period, which ends when he reaches sexual maturity around six to 14 months of age. During the juvenile period he needs to be introduced to strangers (adults, children and other dogs) on the home property. At sexual maturity he will begin to bark at strangers and become more protective. Males start to lift their legs to urinate but if you desire you can inhibit this behavior by walking your boy on leash away from trees, shrubs, fences, etc.

Perhaps you are thinking about an older puppy. You need to inquire about the puppy's social experience. If he has lived in a kennel, he may have a hard time adjusting to people and

Start socializing your Golden at an early age so he feels comfortable around people and other dogs.

environmental stimuli. Assuming he has had a good social upbringing, there are advantages to an older puppy.

Training includes puppy kindergarten and a minimum of one to two basic training classes. During these classes you will learn how to dominate your youngster. This is especially important if you own a large breed of dog. It is somewhat harder, if not nearly impossible, for some owners to be the Alpha figure when their dog towers over them. You will be taught how to properly restrain your dog. This concept is

A properly socialized Golden Retriever should adapt well to an unfamiliar setting, even if he is among strangers and other dogs.

important. Again it puts you in the Alpha position. All dogs need to be restrained many times during their lives. Believe it or not, some of our worst offenders are the eight-week-old puppies that are brought to our clinic. They need to be gently restrained for a nail trim but the way they carry on you would think we were killing them. In comparison, their vaccination is a "piece of cake." When we ask dogs to do something that is not agreeable to them, then their worst comes out. Life will be easier for your dog if you expose him at a young age to the necessities of life—proper behavior and restraint.

Understanding the Dog's Language

Most authorities agree that the dog is a descendent of the wolf. The dog and wolf have similar traits. For instance both are pack oriented and prefer not to be isolated for long periods of time. Another characteristic is that the dog, like the wolf, looks to the leader—Alpha—for direction. Both the wolf and the dog communicate through body language, not only within their pack but with outsiders.

Every pack has an Alpha figure. The dog looks to you, or should look to you, to be that leader. If your dog doesn't receive the proper training and guidance, he very well may replace you as Alpha. This would be a serious problem and is certainly a disservice to your dog.

Eye contact is one way the Alpha wolf keeps order within his pack. You are the Alpha so you must establish eye contact with your puppy. Obviously your puppy will have to look at you. Practice eye contact even if you need to hold his head for five to ten seconds at a time. You can give him a treat as a reward. Make sure your eye contact is gentle and not threatening. Later, if he has been naughty, it is permissible to give him a long, penetrating look. I caution you there are some older dogs that never learned eye contact as puppies and cannot accept eye contact. You should avoid eye contact with these dogs since they feel threatened and will retaliate as such.

BODY LANGUAGE

The play bow, when the forequarters are down and the hindquarters are elevated, is an invitation to play. Puppies play fight, which helps them learn the acceptable limits of biting. This is necessary for later in their lives. Nevertheless, an owner may be falsely reassured by the playful nature of his dog's aggression. Playful aggression toward another dog or human may be an indication of serious aggression in the future. Owners should never play fight or play tug-of-war with any dog that is inclined to be dominant.

Signs of submission are:

1. Avoids eye contact.
2. Active submission—the dog crouches down, ears back and the tail is lowered.
3. Passive submission—the dog rolls on his side with his hindlegs in the air and frequently urinates.

Signs of dominance are:

1. Makes eye contact.
2. Stands with ears up, tail up and the hair raised on his neck.
3. Shows dominance over another dog by standing at right angles over it.

Dominant dogs tend to behave in characteristic ways such as:

1. The dog may be unwilling to move from his place (i.e., reluctant to give up the sofa if the owner wants to sit there).
2. He may not part with toys or objects in his mouth and may show possessiveness with his food bowl.
3. He may not respond quickly to commands.
4. He may be disagreeable for grooming and dislikes to be petted.

Dogs are popular because of their sociable nature. Those that have contact with humans during the first 12 weeks of life regard them as a member of their own species—their pack. All dogs have the potential for both dominant and submissive behavior. Only through experience and training do they learn to whom it is appropriate to show which behavior. Not all dogs are concerned with dominance but owners need to be aware of that potential. It is wise for the owner to establish his dominance early on.

A human can express dominance or submission toward a dog in the following ways:

1. Meeting the dog's gaze signals dominance. Averting the gaze signals submission. If the dog growls or threatens, averting the gaze is the first avoiding action to take—it may prevent attack. It is important to establish eye contact in the puppy. The older dog that has not been exposed to eye contact may see it as a threat and will not be willing to submit.

If actions speak louder than words, this Golden's body language is making quite a statement! Owners, the Morales family.

2. Being taller than the dog signals dominance; being lower signals submission. This is why, when attempting to make friends with a strange dog or catch the runaway, one should kneel down to his level. Some owners see their dogs become dominant when allowed on the furniture or on the bed. Then he is at the owner's level.

3. An owner can gain dominance by ignoring all the dog's social initiatives. The owner pays attention to the dog only when he obeys a command.

No dog should be allowed to achieve dominant status over any adult or child. Ways of preventing are as follows:

1. Handle the puppy gently, especially during the three- to four-month period.

2. Let the children and adults handfeed him and teach him to take food without lunging or grabbing.

3. Do not allow him to chase children or joggers.

4. Do not allow him to jump on people or mount their legs. Even females may be inclined to mount. It is not only a male habit.

5. Do not allow him to growl for any reason.

6. Don't participate in wrestling or tug-of-war games.

7. Don't physically punish puppies for aggressive behavior. Restrain him from repeating the infraction and teach an alternative behavior. Dogs should earn everything they receive from their owners. This would include sitting to receive petting or treats, sitting before going out the door and sitting to receive the collar and leash. These types of exercises reinforce the owner's dominance.

Young children should never be left alone with a dog. It is important that children learn some basic obedience commands so they have some control over the dog. They will gain the respect of their dog.

FEAR

One of the most common problems dogs experience is being fearful. Some dogs are more afraid than others. On the lesser side, which is sometimes humorous to watch, my dog can be afraid of a strange object. He acts silly when something is out of place in the house. I call his problem perceptive intelligence. He realizes the abnormal within his known environment. He does not react the same way in strange environments since he does not know what is normal.

Puppies should be curious and eager to explore—they should not show fear around other dogs.

On the more serious side is a fear of people. This can result in backing off, seeking his own space and saying "leave me alone" or it can result in an aggressive behavior that may lead to challenging the person. Respect that the dog wants to be left alone and give him time to come forward. If you approach the cornered dog, he may resort to snapping. If you leave him alone, he may decide to come forward, which should be rewarded with a treat. Years ago we had a dog that behaved in this manner. We coaxed people to stop by the house and make friends with our fearful dog.

Making eye contact with your dog and being taller than your dog are ways to establish yourself as the "leader of the pack."

She learned to take the treats and after weeks of work she overcame her suspicions and made friends more readily.

Some dogs may initially be too fearful to take treats. In these cases it is helpful to make sure the dog hasn't eaten for about 24 hours. Being a little hungry encourages him to accept the treats, especially if they are of the "gourmet" variety. I have a dog that worries about strangers since people seldom stop by my house. Over the years she has learned a cue and jumps up quickly to visit anyone sitting on the sofa. She learned by herself that all guests on the sofa were to be trusted friends. I think she felt more comfortable with them being at her level, rather than towering over her.

Dogs can be afraid of numerous things, including loud noises and thunderstorms. Invariably the owner rewards (by comforting) the dog when it shows signs of fearfulness. I had a terrible problem with my favorite dog in the Utility obedience class. Not only was he intimidated in the class but he was afraid of noise and afraid of displeasing me. Frequently he would knock down the bar jump, which clattered dreadfully. I gave him credit because he continued to try to clear it, although he was terribly scared. I finally learned to "reward" him every time he knocked down the jump. I would jump up and down, clap my hands and tell him how great he was. My psychology worked, he relaxed and eventually cleared the jump with ease. When your dog is frightened, direct his attention to something else and act happy. Don't dwell on his fright.

AGGRESSION

Some different types of aggression are: predatory, defensive, dominance, possessive, protective, fear induced, noise provoked, "rage" syndrome (unprovoked aggression), maternal and aggression directed toward other dogs. Aggression is the most common behavioral problem encountered. Protective breeds are expected to be more aggressive than others but with the proper upbringing they can make very dependable companions. You need to be able to read your dog.

It's easy to see why the friendly, lovable Golden Retriever is one of the most popular breeds around!

Many factors contribute to aggression including genetics and environment. An improper environment, which may include the living conditions, lack of social life, excessive punishment, being attacked or frightened by an aggressive dog, etc., can all influence a dog's behavior. Even spoiling him and giving too much praise may be detrimental. Isolation and the lack of human contact or exposure to frequent teasing by children or adults also can ruin a good dog.

Lack of direction, fear, or confusion lead to aggression in those dogs that are so inclined. Any obedience exercise, even the sit and down, can direct the dog and overcome fear and/or confusion. Every dog should learn these commands as a youngster, and there should be periodic reinforcement.

When a dog is showing signs of aggression, you should speak calmly (no screaming or hysterics) and firmly give a command that he understands, such as the sit. As soon as your dog obeys, you have assumed your dominant position. Aggression presents a problem because there may be danger to others. Sometimes it is an emotional issue. Owners may consciously or unconsciously encourage their dog's aggression. Other owners show responsibility by accepting the problem and taking measures to keep it under control. The owner is responsible for his dog's actions, and it is not wise to take a chance on someone being bitten, especially a child. Euthanasia is the solution for some owners and in severe cases this may be

the best choice. However, few dogs are that dangerous and very few are that much of a threat to their owners. If caution is exercised and professional help is gained early on, then I surmise most cases can be controlled.

Some authorities recommend feeding a lower protein (less than 20 percent) diet. They believe this can aid in reducing aggression. If the dog loses weight, then vegetable oil can be added. Veterinarians and behaviorists are having some success with pharmacology. In many cases treatment is possible and can improve the situation.

If you have done everything according to "the book" regarding training and socializing and are still having a behavior problem, don't procrastinate. It is important that the problem gets attention before it is out of hand. It is estimated that 20 percent of a veterinarian's time may be devoted to dealing with problems before they become so intolerable that the dog is separated from its home and owner. If your veterinarian isn't able to help, he should refer you to a behaviorist.

It is always wise to invest some time and effort into working on your dog's behavior, but remember—dogs will be dogs!

My most important advice to you is to be aware of your dog's actions. Even so, remember dogs are dogs and will behave as such even though we might like them to be perfect little people. You and your dog will become neurotic if you worry about every little indiscretion. When there is reason for concern—don't waste time. Seek guidance. Dogs are meant to be loved and enjoyed.

References:

Manual of Canine Behavior, Valerie O'Farrell, British Small Animal Veterinary Association.

Good Owners, Great Dogs, Brian Kilcommons, Warner Books.

SUGGESTED READING

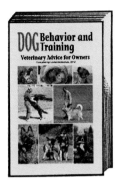

TS-252
Dog Behavior and Training
288 pages, nearly 200 color photos.

TS-249
Skin & Coat Care for Your Dog
224 pages, 300 color photos.

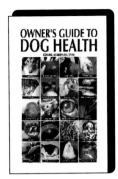

TS-214
Owner's Guide to Dog Health
432 pages, 300 color photos.

TS-205
Successful Dog Training
160 pages, 130 color photos.

TS-258
Training Your Dog For Sports and Other Activities
160 pages, over 200 color photos.

H-1058
Book of the Golden Retriever
480 pages, black and white photos.

PS-786
The Golden Retriever
256 pages, black and white photos.

TS-197
The World of the Golden Retriever
480 pages, over 700 full color photos.

INDEX